WITHDRAWN

COUNTRY
MUSIC

A UNIQUELY
AMERICAN
SOUND

By Tamra B. Orr

Portions of this book originally appeared in
The History of Country Music by Stuart A. Kallen.

THE MUSIC LIBRARY

LUCENT
PRESS

Published in 2019 by
Lucent Press, an Imprint of Greenhaven Publishing, LLC
353 3rd Avenue
Suite 255
New York, NY 10010

Designer: Deanna Paternostro
Editor: Siyavush Saidian

Library of Congress Cataloging-in-Publication Data

Names: Orr, Tamra B., author.
Title: Country music : a uniquely American sound / Tamra B. Orr.
Description: New York : Lucent Press, [2019] | Includes bibliographical
  references and index.
Identifiers: LCCN 2018025657 (print) | LCCN 2018025754 (ebook) | ISBN
  9781534565197 (eBook) | ISBN 9781534565180 (library bound book) | ISBN
  9781534565173 (pbk. book)
Subjects: LCSH: Country music–History and criticism.
Classification: LCC ML3521 (ebook) | LCC ML3521 .S22 2019 (print) | DDC
  781.642–dc23
LC record available at https://lccn.loc.gov/2018025657

Printed in the United States of America

CPSIA compliance information: Batch #BW19KL: For further information contact Greenhaven Publishing LLC,
New York, New York at 1-844-317-7404.

Please visit our website, www.greenhavenpublishing.com. For a free color catalog of all our high-quality books,
call toll free 1-844-317-7404 or fax 1-844-317-7405.

Table of
Contents

Foreword

Music has a unique ability to speak to people on a deeply personal level and to bring people together. Whether it is experienced through playing a favorite song on a smartphone or at a live concert surrounded by thousands of screaming fans, music creates a powerful connection that sends songs to the top of the charts and artists to the heights of fame.

Music history traces the evolution of those songs and artists. Each generation of musicians builds on the one that came before, and a strong understanding of the artists of the past can help inspire the musical superstars of the future to continue to push boundaries and break new ground.

A closer look at the history of a musical genre also reveals its impact on culture and world events. Music has inspired social change and ignited cultural revolutions. It does more than simply reflect the world; it helps to shape the world.

Music is often considered a universal language. A great song or album speaks to people regardless of age, race, economic status, or nationality. Music from various artists, genres, countries, and time periods might seem completely different at first, but certain themes can be found in all kinds of music: love and loss, success and failure, and life and death. In discovering these similarities, music fans are able to see how many things we all have in common.

Each style of music has its own story, and those stories are filled with colorful characters, shocking events, and songs with true staying power. The Music Library presents those stories to readers with the help of those who know the stories best—music critics, historians, and artists. Annotated quotes by these experts give readers an inside look at a wide variety of musical styles— from early hip-hop and classic country to today's chart-topping pop hits and indie rock favorites. Readers with a passion for music—whether they are headbangers or lovers of

Latin music—will discover fun facts about their favorite artists and gain a deeper appreciation for how those artists were influenced by the ones who paved the way in the past.

The Music Library is also designed to serve as an accessible introduction to unfamiliar genres. Suggestions for additional books and websites to explore for more information inspire readers to dive even further into the topics, and the essential albums in each genre are compiled for superfans and new listeners to enjoy. Photographs of some of music's biggest names of the past and present fill the pages, placing readers in the middle of music history.

All music tells a story. Those stories connect people from different places, cultures, and time periods. In understanding the history of the stories told through music, readers discover an exciting way of looking at the past and develop a deeper appreciation for different voices.

Country Music
Then and Now

Most people who hear the term "country music" immediately think of songs about beloved trucks, special dogs, cheating partners, cherished families, and love of the United States. They imagine singers in cowboy hats, leather boots, and tight jeans strumming guitars or banjos. However, where once listeners might have just thought of country music performers as being found on the stages of Nashville, Tennessee, or on all-country radio stations, that is no longer true. Modern country music artists may sing about some of the same themes, but they are doing it for a much wider audience and merging with big rock beats and seamless digital production. Their songs top the country charts—but also break into the Billboard charts for non-country music.

While the songs from top country artists in the digital age are being downloaded frequently, the origin of country music can be traced back to the 1930s to 1950s. Modern country music from such artists as Miranda Lambert, Carrie Underwood, and Luke Bryan all reach back decades to the sweet gospel-tinged harmonies of the Carter Family, the bluegrass mandolin of Bill Monroe, the fiddle arrangements of Bob Wills, and the lonesome love songs of Hank Williams.

Appalachian Music

When English and Scotch-Irish immigrants first moved into the green rolling hills of the southern Appalachian Mountains in the mid-1700s, they carried just the basics: clothing, food, and their fiddles, guitars, and mandolins. It was a difficult journey across rocky terrain, and once the travelers had settled in, they and their descendants found themselves quite isolated. Singing and playing music was a way to not only be entertained, but also to bond with others. Ancient English and Irish songs were shared by all as a way to remember their homelands.

The isolation of the Appalachian

people came to an end with the start of the 20th century. The rolling hills in the South were changed by train tracks, coal mines, textile mills, iron and steel mills, and oil fields. Instead of spending their days hunting, fishing, and farming, people found themselves digging in mines, punching factory clocks, and laboring on trains and drilling rigs. The changes from this lifestyle rippled out, impacting everything from sleep schedules to music themes. Now, lyrics spoke less of new opportunities and lands and more of broken hearts and low wages.

The songs of Appalachia spread across America, pushed along in part by the growing use of radio and record players. These tunes were

Playing instruments as a family gave many people a chance to relax and spend time together.

Luke Bryan is a familiar face to country music fans,
whether in concert, winning an award, or on reality television.

rooted in the thoughts and dreams of hardworking, patriotic people. At first, the music style was called "hillbilly" music. Others called it old-time, oat tunes, or folk. Finally, in 1949, the term "country and western" music was used. As country music spread and more musicians began singing and playing, the songs divided into certain styles, including bluegrass, western swing, honky-tonk, and the Nashville sound. Since then, the styles have expanded even further, merging with the sounds of pop, rock, and blues. Today, people enjoy country pop, Americana, neotraditionalism, and alternative or alt-country.

Country music has grown in a number of directions over time. Country Music Television (CMT) was first introduced in the mid-1980s. It featured videos, concerts, movies, documentaries, and programs for country fans. Decades later, it is still a favorite with country music fans. In 2016, Jayson Dinsmore, former executive vice president of CMT development, stated, "Our format may change, our shows may change, but our core values will remain the same. It's all driven by the sensibilities of our biggest stars."[1] Since the early 1990s, the internet has featured dozens of stations with country music playlists, including bluegrass, up-tempo dance, classics, contemporary, outlaw, and more. In the 2000s, anyone with internet access could download contemporary country albums or classic tunes dating back an entire century.

Today, country music remains a big business. In 2016, 10 percent of all album sales were country music artists, including Chris Stapleton, Garth Brooks, and Blake Shelton. Live concerts continue to be one of the most profitable venues for country music artists, along with selling or endorsing various products. For example, between June 2016 and June 2017, Kenny Chesney earned $42.5 million by filling up stadiums and doing commercials for various products, including computers. Luke Bryan was close behind with $42 million between his concerts and his appearances on the reality television show *Buck Commander*. Bryan has also served as a judge on the hit television series *American Idol*.

While country music has changed a great deal over time, many maintain that the music's original goal—being a healing tonic for anyone with a broken heart, the lonesome blues, or just the need to connect with others—has changed very little since those early days in the Appalachian Mountains.

CHAPTER ONE

Early
Country Music

In the early 20th century, a man named Ralph Peer had a unique gift. He had the ability to hear a type of music and know whether it was marketable or not. He worked for the recording industry in New York City. In 1923, when a local record dealer suggested Peer take a trip to Atlanta, Georgia, to hear a fiddle player named John Carson, Peer was intrigued. He had heard about Victor Records fiddlers Eck Robertson and Henry Gilliland. Their fiddle tunes "Sallie Gooden" and "Arkansas Traveler" had just been released on Victor's label. Other songs, including "It Ain't Gonna Rain No Mo," were rising on the charts. Peer knew he had to get involved in this style of music—and fast.

In June, Peer was in Atlanta, listening to Carson play "The Little Old Log Cabin in the Lane" and "The Old Hen Cackled and the Rooster's Going to Crow." He thought the music was awful. However, other people disagreed. They thought "Fiddlin'" John Carson was amazing. Peer recorded the man's music, along with music of other "hillbilly" musicians. People loved it—and country music began to spread.

In the summer of 1927, Peer went to Bristol, Tennessee, to hold a very special on-site recording session. Some music historians believe that moment was a turning point for country music, as Peer recorded a variety of musicians for 12 days. Two of the acts—Jimmie Rodgers and the Carter Family—were about to become music legends.

Early Legends

Anyone stopping by the Carter Fold in southwest Virginia on Saturday nights can hear the sounds of guitars, banjos, and harmony filling the air. For decades, the Carter Fold has been featuring weekly concerts in the grand tradition of the original Carter Family, one of the biggest legends in early country music. As their website states, "A Saturday with us in rural southwest Virginia will supply you with an evening of musical entertainment and country hospitality you won't soon forget. Chances are you'll make some new friends and take with you some fond memories."[2]

According to the 2014 documentary *The Winding Stream*, in the early 20th century, a young Alvin P. Carter, known as A. P., was going door-to-door trying to sell fruit trees. As he walked, A. P. was distracted by the sounds of a young woman named Sara Dougherty singing and playing the autoharp. The two began talking—and not long after, they were married. A. P., along with Sara and his sister-in-law Maybelle, traveled to Bristol in 1927 to perform and record for Peer. Their song, "Single Girl, Married Girl" was a hit and was soon selling records. The Carter Family's sound was unique because it was based less on musical instruments and more on vocals. The trio had amazing three-part harmonies, and A. P. wrote most of the group's material. These songs, including "Wildwood Flower," "I'm Thinking Tonight of My Blue Eyes," "Will the Circle Be Unbroken," and "Hello Stranger," sold millions of records. The Carter Family songs are country standards that are still sung

The Carter Family was so popular that their music was arranged and printed in songbooks so fans could learn their favorite songs.

today. Sara Carter was the first female country music star. Maybelle's technique of thumb picking her guitar, later known as Carter picking, made the guitar a lead instrument for the first time. Although the group disbanded in the early 1940s, their music influenced a generation of country and rock musicians in the following decades. When Maybelle died in 1978, experts noted that the Carter Family made great strides in reviving interest in traditional European folk songs in America.

Filling Airtime

When the first commercial radio station went on the air in 1920, it changed the country—and its music. By the end of 1923, there were more than 550 broadcasting stations in the United States, and each one was scrambling to fill hours of airtime. In the South, scouts searched taverns and theaters for country music performers. One of the most popular country singers of the era, Eddy Arnold, was hired by agents while he was playing music on his front porch.

By 1924, listeners across the country could tune in on Saturday nights to the powerful 50,000-watt AM radio station WLS in Chicago, Illinois, to hear the *National Barn Dance*. This wildly popular radio show featured romantic country crooners, foot-tapping string

bands, yodeling cowboys, cornball comics, and even barbershop quartets singing slick four-part harmonies. In 1932, the show was picked up by NBC and broadcast on dozens of stations from coast to coast. *National Barn Dance* made stars out of performers Bradley Kincaid, Grandpa Jones, and cowgirl singer Patsy Montana—the first female country solo artist to sell 1 million records. The show also inspired a new group of country musicians who were amazed at what was possible through radio broadcasting.

The success of *National Barn Dance* inspired the creation of dozens of similar shows throughout the country. None were as popular or enduring as the *Grand Ole Opry* on WSM in Nashville. When the show went on the air on November 28, 1925, people were able to hear it across a wide region because of WSM's powerful signal. The show was on the air for almost two years before it was officially named. After a formal program of classical opera music, announcer George D. Hay came on the air and said, "For the past hour you have been listening to music taken largely from the Grand Opera, but from now on we will present the Grand Ole Opry."[3]

By the late 1930s, the star of the *Grand Ole Opry* was the fiddler and singer Roy Acuff, sometimes called the King of Country Music. Acuff's band, the Smoky Mountain

Four couples are shown here dancing during a recording of the National Barn Dance *program. The program inspired the creation of many shows such as the* Grand Ole Opry.

Boys, was the first to feature a Dobro, the name given to a slide guitar that looks similar to a regular guitar with a metal piece that looks like a car hubcap attached to the face of the instrument. This metal resonator makes the Dobro louder than an average guitar. The ringing Dobro blended well with Acuff's hard-charging singing style. His hits, such as "The Great Speckled Bird," "Wabash Cannonball," "Wreck on the Highway," and "I Saw the Light," became instant country standards.

Performers on the Grand Ole Opry *often dressed up to fit their country style.*

Roy Acuff and the *Grand Ole Opry* helped make Nashville the country music capital of the world. Over the years, the venue has changed, but today it continues to draw crowds to its stages with modern stars, including the Band Perry, Luke Bryan, Brad Paisley, and Carrie Underwood.

Bill Monroe and his Blue Grass Boys

In 1938, a mandolin player from Kentucky named Bill Monroe auditioned for the *Grand Ole Opry*. He played Jimmie Rodgers's "Mule Skinner Blues," backed by his band, the Blue Grass Boys. George D. Hay and Harry Stone, the *Grand Ole Opry*'s producers, were astounded by Monroe's lightning-fast licks, and they hired him on the spot. According to Monroe, the producers told him, "I had more perfect music for the station than any music they'd ever heard."[4] Radio listeners agreed, and Bill Monroe and the Blue Grass Boys were soon among the show's most popular players.

Today, Monroe is considered the founding father of bluegrass music. The style depends on quick cascades of improvised notes, often made up by the player on the spot. A standard bluegrass band, such as Monroe's, consisted of five pieces: violin, mandolin, guitar, banjo, and stand-up bass. Other bluegrass bands occasionally add harmonica, piano, or Dobro to the mix. Monroe's group also pioneered four-part bluegrass vocal harmony. George D. Hay described Monroe's unique voice: "There is that authentic wail in his high-pitched voice that one hears in the evening in the country when Mother Nature sighs and retires for the night."[5] Monroe himself described his band's harmony as that "high, lonesome sound."[6]

Playing on the *Grand Ole Opry* in the early 1940s helped make Bill Monroe and the Blue Grass Boys national stars. Monroe was not satisfied, however. As he recalled in 1993, "I wanted a style of music of my own … [and] I was going to play it the way I thought it should be played."[7] In 1945, Monroe put together an all-star band that would become synonymous with the genre of bluegrass. After hiring guitarist Lester Flatt, banjo picker Earl Scruggs, fiddler Chubby Wise, and bassist Howard "Cedric Rainwater" Watts, his new Blue Grass Boys burned up the stage at the *Grand Ole Opry* during the live shows.

Long before it was common for musicians to have legions of dedicated, passionate fans, the Blue Grass Boys were a country music phenomenon. The audience screamed and yelled when the band played their bluegrass "breakdowns" (songs played in double time). On tour, the band broke attendance records wherever they went. Young musicians played the band's records at slower speeds on their phonographs, desperately trying to imitate the red-hot picking styles of Monroe and other band members. The musical style became so popular that by 1953, almost every southern town had at least one amateur bluegrass band.

Today, Monroe's songs—including "Blue Moon of Kentucky," "Uncle Pen," "In the Pines," "Molly and Tenbrooks," and "My Sweet Blue-Eyed Darlin'"—are bluegrass standards beloved by both musicians and fans. As to the secret of his success, Monroe stated plainly, "You always play it the best way you can … Play it good and clean and play good melodies with it, and keep perfect time. It takes really good timing with bluegrass music, and it takes some good high voices to really deliver it right."[8]

The father of bluegrass music died in 1996—just before his 85th birthday. By then, Monroe had seen his unique style adapted by countless players throughout the United States, Europe, and beyond. The reach of his bluegrass style was also extended by the dozens of gifted musicians who played with his Blue Grass Boys over the years.

In 1948, Blue Grass Boys Lester Flatt, Earl Scruggs, and Howard Watts formed a band called the Foggy Mountain Boys. Scruggs was a popular musician, and, as bluegrass musician and author Bob Artis wrote, "Audiences just couldn't believe that anyone could play the banjo like Earl Scruggs. It was so fast and smooth, and there were so many notes, but all the melody and everything else was right there in the shower of banjo music. The crowds would roar every time Earl stepped to the microphone."[9]

Much of the thrill was the sound of the lightning fast, three-finger picking style that Scruggs had perfected since he started playing the banjo in North Carolina at the age of four. In 1949, Scruggs wrote "Foggy Mountain Breakdown." The song became an instant classic in every banjo player's repertoire. In 1967, it was used as the theme song for the hit movie *Bonnie and Clyde*.

By the late 1950s, the Foggy Mountain Boys were taking their brand of blistering bluegrass breakdowns beyond the traditional country circuit to college campuses, where a new generation was eager to hear their sound. In 1962, Scruggs wrote "The Ballad of Jed Clampett," the theme song for the hit television comedy *The Beverly Hillbillies*. Scruggs appeared on the extremely popular show numerous times with Lester Flatt, making Flatt and Scruggs household names, even for those who were not bluegrass fans.

The popularity of bluegrass music during the 1960s was nurtured by the number of music festivals popping up across the country. The first festival was held on July 4, 1961, in a park in Luray, Virginia. It was the first time that an entire festival was dedicated solely to multiple artists playing bluegrass. The Luray festival featured Bill Monroe, the Stanley Brothers, Jim & Jesse, and the Country Gentlemen. The event quickly sold thousands of tickets—a huge number at the time—and the new venue for bluegrass music became an annual event.

In 1967, Monroe held his own festival in Bean Blossom, Indiana, a place he often played in his early years. The first events had fewer than 5,000 people in attendance. By the 1980s, Bean Blossom had grown into one of the largest celebrations of bluegrass music in the world. The festival celebrated its

PICK WISELY

One of the distinctive features of bluegrass music is the way the banjo strings are picked. For many guitar players, the only way to play is by holding a single plastic pick between their thumb and forefinger to hit the strings of their instrument. Earl Scruggs, however, revolutionized banjo playing with his unique picking techniques:

> Scruggs is probably the best-known banjo picker in the world. And even people who don't know his name know what is called the Scruggs style of playing when they hear it: a crackling, syncopated style in which the player uses the thumb and two fingers fitted with plastic and metal picks to play chords, melody and cascading rolls of notes.

> Scruggs recalls that a crisp finger picking style with thumb and forefinger or a thumb and two fingers—similar to classical guitar playing—was the most common way to play the five-string banjo in his western North Carolina hometown ...

> Earl started to play [banjo] before he was even big enough to hold it. He started with just the thumb and forefinger, but one day when he was about 10 years old, something new happened ...

> "I'd gone into a room by myself, and I had the banjo in there ... And all of a sudden, I realized I was picking with three fingers. And that excited me to no end."[1]

The rest of the country music world agreed with Scruggs—his new techniques were captivating to countless crowds as he launched an extremely successful musical career.

1. Quoted in Paul Brown, "The Story of 'Foggy Mountain Breakdown,'" NPR, April 1, 2000. www.npr.org/2000/04/01/1072355/npr-100-earl-scruggs.

52nd birthday in 2018, making it the oldest continuously running bluegrass festival anywhere as of that date. Held for 8 days during the summer, it features more than 70 bands, and thousands of people come to listen. Today, hundreds of bluegrass festivals are held worldwide. Nearly every state hosts a festival, and celebrations of bluegrass music are also found in Japan, England, and elsewhere.

Doc Watson and *MerleFest*

The distinguished guitar picker Arthel "Doc" Watson is another bluegrass picker who gained recognition at 1960s bluegrass festivals. His name is synonymous with bluegrass guitar wizardry, impressive musical chops, and undeniable influence.

Watson was born in Deep Gap, North Carolina, in 1923. He was blind since infancy. Like many pickers, he came from a musical family, and he taught himself how to play the guitar as a teenager. Watson played rockabilly and western swing until his 30s. Because his band did not have a fiddle player, Watson learned to pick out the complicated old-time songs on his guitar. He played the fiddle tunes "flat pick" style, or with a single guitar pick—as opposed to Earl Scruggs's famous finger picks.

When renowned folklorist Ralph Rinzler heard Watson play, he immediately began booking him at festivals and folk clubs. In 1963, Watson landed a coveted spot at the *Newport Folk Festival*. In later years, Watson toured with his son Eddy Merle, another hot guitar picker, who died in a tractor accident in 1985.

Three years after Eddy Merle's tragic death, his father held a series of benefit concerts in Wilkesboro, North Carolina, to raise money for the local community. The first *MerleFest* used two flatbed trucks for stages. Since then, *Merlefest* has grown into one of America's premier bluegrass and country music festivals. The 4-day event includes 13 stages featuring more than 100 acts—from Dolly Parton and Alison Krauss to Steve Martin and the Steep Canyon Rangers.

Each year, about 75,000 adults and children attend the festival. "That's about the size every year, and our goal has never been to see how big we could get," *MerleFest* director Ted Hagaman said. "There are limitations with roads, hotels, infrastructure. So it's more about maintaining the quality of the event, making sure everyone who comes feels like they get their money's worth. If we keep our eye on that ball, everything else will take care of itself."[10] In addition to bringing more than $10 million to the local economy, this bluegrass paradise distributes millions of dollars to civic and charitable organizations.

In spring 2018, the International Bluegrass Music Museum in Owensboro, Kentucky, was renamed the Bluegrass Hall of Fame and Museum. "It's more than a name change," explained executive director Chris Joslin. "This new branding sets the stage for the

Doc Watson (right) honored his son by frequently performing at MerleFest.

October grand opening of our new facility."[11] In autumn 2018, the museum hosted a grand opening, with visitors enjoying live music, special guests, and exhibit openings. The mission of the facility is simple: to be the world center for the presentation of the history, culture, and future of bluegrass music. It is the realization of a vision that the countless bluegrass fans across the generations want—and appreciate.

CHAPTER TWO

Cowboys and
Western Swing

As people gathered around their radios to listen to the latest song being performed on the *Grand Ole Opry*, another style of western music was evolving and expanding. Cowboys had been a part of the nation's storytelling tradition for decades. The Wild West figures were found in novels and stories, their adventures thrilling audiences of all ages. Their allure had spilled over onto the movie screen, and performers such as Gene Autry, Tex Ritter, and Roy Rogers were drawing countless moviegoers to the theater. During the Great Depression in the 1930s, money was scarce, jobs were impossible to find, and people were scared. People singing on and off horseback in westerns made these rough times more bearable. Just as European countries had folk stories about knights, cowboy stories became a way for many Americans to escape the reality of their lives during the Great Depression.

Finding Fame

In the 1930s, dozens of cowboy bands and individual artists with names such as the Lonesome Cowboy, the Sons of the Pioneers, Cowboy Slim, and the Girls of the Golden West took advantage of the demand for cowboy acts. Most had never roped a steer, mended a fence, or chased off a cattle thief. The Sons of the Pioneers were led by Leonard Slye. He was a former factory worker and truck driver who grew up in a crowded, run-down apartment in Ohio. Leonard Slye was not noteworthy, however, until he changed his name to Roy Rogers in 1938. He made more than 100 movies and earned the title King of the Cowboys (taken from the name of one of his popular movies).

Unlike some, Jules Verne Allen, also known as Longhorn Luke, was a real cowboy. As a young man, Allen worked on a cattle ranch in Waxahachie, Texas. He

Roy Rogers was a singing cowboy who rarely went anywhere without his loyal horse, Trigger.

later became a broncobuster— someone who tames wild horses so they can be ready for the saddle—in Montana. Throughout the 1930s, Allen performed on radio stations in the West, calling himself the Original Singing Cowboy. He recorded songs such as "The Cow Trail to Mexico," "Little Joe, the Wrangler," and "The Cowboy's Dream." When western movies grew popular, Allen was skeptical of

Movies featuring singing cowboys, such as Gene Autry, were a big hit with audiences during the Great Depression.

them. "It's rather remarkable that the cowboy of fiction and movie fame does everything except caring for cattle,"[12] he stated, clearly mocking his less authentic counterparts.

Goebel Reeves, also called the Texas Drifter, was another cowboy who sang from experience. Although his father was in the Texas legislature, Reeves chose to live without a home and ride the rails. Like other drifters during the Great Depression, Reeves encountered hunger, isolation, brutal railroad detectives, and cold prison cells. This gave a genuine voice to the songs he wrote, including "Hobo's Lullaby," "The Cowboy's Dream," and "The Hobo and the Cop."

Hollywood film directors were quick to pick up on the singing cowboy trend. The first genuine horse-riding musician to appear on the silver screen was trick rider Ken Maynard, who sang traditional trailside songs such as "The Lone Star Trail."

Gene Autry, the superstar of the singing cowboys, was originally a telegraph operator for the railroad in Sapulpa, Oklahoma. In 1929, after being discovered by comedian Will Rogers, Autry signed a recording contract with Columbia Records. Autry's claim to fame was that he could closely imitate Jimmie Rodgers's yodeling style. Finally, Autry recorded some records, including the song "That Silver-Haired Daddy of Mine." It earned him a spot on Chicago's influential WLS *National Barn Dance* radio show. Autry became an overnight sensation, and by 1934, he was in Hollywood making movies, billed as the "Nation's Number One Singing Cowboy."[13] Autry eventually made more than 100 films and became the most famous singing cowboy in the world. As Don Cusic, author of *The Cowboy in Country Music*, said,

He was like a breath of fresh air. The movie people didn't like him—they thought he was too feminine, not masculine enough to be a cowboy hero. But he had an appealing voice, he had that presence, he kind of had that "next-door" look, and he was a great singer. One of the things he did in his movies was put the old West in the contemporary West. People rode horses, but they also drove pick-up trucks. They chased bad guys, but they also had a telephone and a phonograph.[14]

Autry was so popular that Hollywood producers began searching for other cowboy acts. Dozens of country bands dropped their traditional tunes, bought cowboy outfits, and adopted names such

A WANDERER'S LIFESTYLE

Harry "Haywire Mac" McClintock was a traveling cowboy songwriter who led a very interesting life, as music journalist Kurt Wolff explained:

McClintock wasn't your average cowboy singer. He wasn't your average anything, in fact. Born in Knoxville, Tennessee, in 1882, he left home as a teenager to ride the rails and see the world ... In addition to making music, he held an assortment of odd jobs during his lifetime, including cowboy, mule driver, seaman and journalist. "Haywire Mac," a nickname he picked up along the way, recorded more than forty sides for Victor, but he became well known as a pioneering radio personality ...

Mac's hobo songs ... were gritty and unflinching on the one hand, yet also presented a good-natured view of the wanderer's lifestyle—which was a common experience at the time, as many young men rode the rails both as a way to see the world and as a means to travel between jobs. ["Hallelujah, Bum Again"] isn't so much a ballad on the perils of homelessness as it is a celebration of the hobo lifestyle—something the protagonist has adopted by choice. "I don't like work, and work don't like me," sings McClintock, "and that is the reason I am so hungry."[1]

1. Kurt Wolff, *Country Music: The Rough Guide*. London, UK: Rough Guides, 2000, pp. 55–56.

as Riders of the Purple Sage or the Cowboy Ramblers.

Enter Cowboy Jazz

Far from Hollywood, in real cowboy country, western music was changing. When Texan music gets mixed with African American jazz and blues, fiddles, urban pop, Mexican mariachi, and Louisiana Cajun music, it creates western swing music, or cowboy jazz. This style of music topped the country charts for nearly 20 years in the early to mid 1900s.

Thanks to its blend of styles, western swing was played with big bands—some with more than a dozen players. A typical 1930s western swing band might include a piano, mandolin, bass, slide guitars, saxophones, drums, and several fiddles, trumpets, and vocalists. While members of western swing bands often wore cowboy boots and Stetson cowboy hats, they were actually playing music that was a spinoff of urban jazz. The country and western tones were added by fiddles and pedal steel guitars and featured lyrics about cities such as San Antonio, Texas; Amarillo, Texas; and Tulsa, Oklahoma.

Bob Wills, from Turkey, Texas, was the king of western swing. From the age of three, Wills worked side by side in the Texas cotton fields with local black musicians who taught him blues and Dixieland jazz. He played his first gig in 1915 when he was just 10 years old: His fiddling father, John, failed to appear at a ranch dance, so young Bob filled in, playing the few songs he knew by heart. The cowpokes, ranch hands, and assembled ladies first laughed at the small boy, but they soon started dancing.

By the time he was 25, Wills was pioneering a unique blend of western jazz—intermingling his fiddle notes with jazz and blues. In 1930, Wills played regularly on radio shows in Fort Worth, Texas. He soon added singer Milton Brown to his Wills Fiddle Band, a pumped-up string band with fiddles, a piano, a banjo, and two guitars. In 1932, when the band landed an important gig on a radio program sponsored by Light Crust Flour, Wills and Brown renamed the group the Light Crust Doughboys.

Although the Doughboys were popular, their success was hampered by Wills. Now and then, he would disappear on weeklong drinking binges, causing the band to miss important engagements. These outbreaks of alcohol abuse were rare—Wills remained sober most of the time. However, on one of those occasions when Wills failed to show up for a radio show, the Doughboys were fired, prompting key band members to quit.

It is quite possible that Bob Wills would have been less famous if one of his main competitors (and former bandmate), Milton Brown, had not died in a 1936 car accident. Brown, backed by Wills on fiddle, was the first to record western swing songs—"Nancy Jane" and "Sunbonnet Sue"—under the band name the Fort Worth Doughboys.

Shortly after leaving the Doughboys, Brown formed the band His Musical Brownies. The group's popularity quickly rivaled that of the Doughboys. The Brownies' sound was boosted by the addition of Bob Dunn, whose electric steel guitar was the first amplified instrument used in country music.

The guitar amplifier, or amp, he played through was a high-tech wonder of the day, since the first amps were developed between the

Paul Tutmarc was the inventor of electrically-amplified steel guitars, which are now a staple in country music.

1920s and 1930s. Brown described his band's sound as combining jazz, hillbilly, and strings. Record producers noticed it immediately, and over the next 4 years, the Brownies recorded more than 100 songs. They even produced 50 songs in a marathon recording session in March 1936. At the same time, the Brownies were making waves in nightclubs and packing in huge crowds. As music journalist Kurt Wolff wrote,

The Brownies' hot, swinging dance music struck a chord with people all over the state who were suffering through the Depression. The music was hot and loose, with a mixture of fiddle, piano and guitar playing, a Dixieland-style rhythm, Dunn's amplified steel and Brown's smooth lead vocals. They played familiar jazz tunes like "St. Louis Blues" … and steaming-hot Mexican-flavored numbers like

"In El Rancho Grande." At his peak Brown's songs were wild, juicy and almost out of control—the instrumentalists firmly tethered to the rhythm, yet at the same time appearing to barely hang on.[15]

Sadly, the Brownies' brand of hot western swing came to a tragic end when Milton Brown was killed in a car accident in 1936. Although the band stayed together for two years after his death, they finally quit playing in 1938.

Music and Controversy

In 1933, after the Light Crust Doughboys broke up, Bob Wills put together Bob Wills and His Texas Playboys. It consisted of Wills on fiddle, a vocalist, pianist, bassist, and a rhythm guitarist. Wills also brought in Leon McAuliffe, who was incredibly skilled with the slide bar on the electric steel guitar. McAuliffe's 1936 composition "Steel Guitar Rag" helped popularize the steel guitar throughout the United States, making it an essential instrument in country bands.

Between 1934 and 1942, the Texas Playboys worked out of Tulsa, playing a continual series of radio and dance shows. In a 1935 recording session in Dallas, Texas, Wills utilized a 13-piece band with a trumpet, saxophone, clarinet, trombone, and trio of violinists. This version of the Texas Playboys was the first to play true to the style that would later be labeled western swing.

At the time, the wild sounds of western swing generated quite a bit of controversy. The Tulsa musicians union refused membership to the Texas Playboys because union bosses ruled that their sound was not music—and so the Playboys were not musicians. Despite this prejudice, the Texas Playboys were some of the hottest—and most entertaining—performers around.

The music of the Texas Playboys was, above all, dance music. It revolved around the fiddles, but Wills focused on projecting an air of musical sophistication and class. The band played blues songs such as "Sittin' on Top of the World," Jimmie Rodgers compositions such as "Blue Yodel No. 1," and jazzy numbers such as "Osage Stomp." Despite this diverse repertoire, the music was fun. Wolff wrote,

For all its sophistication, the Playboys' music was also wild, loose and free of stylistic constraints. When twin fiddles, guitars, horns and drums fired into song, "rowdy" was definitely part of the agenda. The players were superb, and one by one each would take solos that boggled the minds of the spectators and

BOB WILLS
and his TEXAS PLAYBOYS

Bob Wills is shown here with the rest of the Texas Playboys.

dancers. Western swing was all about fun and good times, and Wills' whoops … and interjections of "play that trombone, boy" or "take it away, Leon" when each man stepped to the mike gave the whole experience a playful feeling … Cindy Walker even wrote a song for the Playboys titled "What Makes Bob Holler?" that poked gentle fun at Wills' uninhibited commentary; it became a Playboys standard.[16]

By 1940, with their unique mix of country standards, fiddle tunes, blues, and jazz, the Texas Playboys were competing with popular jazz-based swing bands led by Tommy Dorsey, Glenn Miller, and Benny Goodman. That same year, the Texas Playboys' song "New San Antonio Rose" was stocked in more than 300,000 jukeboxes—coin-operated record players that allowed listeners to hear their favorite songs for a nickel. The song went on to sell 1 million copies. Other early 1940s Texas Playboys hits included "Take Me Back to Tulsa," "Ida Red," and "Let's Ride With Bob."

Like many other singing cowboys, Wills soon made it out to Hollywood, where his entire band appeared in the 1941 film *Go West, Young Lady*. The next year, Wills was hired by Columbia Pictures to appear in eight films. By the late 1940s, Wills was the highest-paid leader of any band in the country. In 1947, he opened his own nightclub—Wills Point—in Sacramento, California. His live shows were broadcast on the radio and heard throughout the West. When the Texas Playboys put on shows in Washington, Oregon, California, Texas, and Arizona, they drew up to 10,000 people a night— huge crowds for that era.

The Importance of Rhythm

In the early 1950s, Bob Wills's fortunes began to fade. His music was considered too sophisticated for country fans after World War II and too country for pop music radio stations. The popularity of western swing took another hit in the mid-1950s when Elvis Presley, Chuck Berry, Jerry Lee Lewis, and Bill Haley and His Comets burst onto the scene. These artists combined country hillbilly sounds with fast-tempo rhythm and blues to create a new style called rockabilly.

Rockabilly, which was popularized by white musicians with country music backgrounds, was a style of rock and roll pioneered in the late 1940s by Wynonie Harris and other African American musicians. Harris's songs, such as "Good Rockin' Tonight," with its shouted vocals, loud hand claps, rollicking piano, and walking bass line, are credited as some of the first rock-and-roll songs.

When American teenagers began buying millions of rock-and-roll and rockabilly records, western swing was all but forgotten. This greatly disappointed Wills. He felt his music had helped lay the foundation for the rock-and-roll revolution. As he told a Tulsa newspaper in 1957,

Rock and Roll? Why, man, that's the same kind of music we've been playin' since 1928! … We didn't call it "rock and roll" back when we introduced it as our style back in 1928, and we don't call it rock

and roll the way we play it now. But it's just basic rhythm and has gone by a lot of different names in my time. It's the same, whether you just follow a drum beat like in Africa or surround it with a lot of instruments. The rhythm's what's important.[17]

BERRY AND ROCKABILLY

In 1955, the innovative guitarist and songwriter Chuck Berry had a number-1 hit with the song "Maybellene." Berry freely admitted that the loping dance beat of the song was based on "Ida Red," a 1938 hit for Bob Wills and His Texas Playboys. Like many other early rock songs, "Maybellene" combined country with boogie-woogie, which features a driving rhythm that originated in churches that were attended mainly by black Americans. The new sound was called rockabilly, one of the earliest types of rock and roll.

In a way, rockabilly was the opposite of western swing. Rockabilly lacked tight arrangements and sophisticated musicianship. While swing bands utilized dozens of virtuoso, or highly skilled, musicians playing advanced jazz licks, rockabilly groups needed nothing more than a singer accompanied by a stand-up "slap" bass, an electric guitar, and a drummer. The exciting new beat of rockabilly was behind early Elvis Presley hits, including "Blue Suede Shoes," and propelled artists such as Gene Vincent and Jerry Lee Lewis to the top of the charts in the second half of the 1950s.

Wills continued to play on occasion, but his declining health in the early 1960s forced him to break up his band. A stroke in 1969 paralyzed his right side, leaving him unable to play. Sensing his time was limited, he assembled the old Texas Playboys for one more recording session in December 1973. The resulting album was the double album *For the Last Time* (later released as a single album). Although they had not played together in years, the Texas Playboys expertly ran through Wills classics such as "Texas Playboy Theme," "What Makes Bob Holler?," "San Antonio Rose," and "Bubbles in My Beer." They were joined on the vocals by country superstar Merle Haggard, a huge Wills fan. Meanwhile, Wills sat in the middle of the room in his wheelchair, beaming with joy and throwing in an occasional shout of encouragement.

After six songs, Wills went home. That same night, he had another stroke and slipped into a coma. The Texas Playboys continued recording, now with new determination to bring the old songs to life again. Wills was still unconscious when *For the Last Time* was released in 1974, but he clung to life until May 1975. Today, *For the Last Time* stands as an unshakable testimony to the man who pioneered western swing.

Western swing's blend of blues, jazz, country, Mexican, and Cajun sounds reflected the changing population of the United States. As people from different states and countries moved around, bringing their traditions, cultures, and skills with them, everything changed—including the music. Many of those influences could be heard in western swing and can still be heard. Western swing festivals are still hosted across the South. In Canton, Texas, the *Legends of Western Swing Music Festival* began in 1987 and is still going today. "We've been going a long time, and we are sort of the granddaddy of the swing shows," producer Gloria Miers said. Performers include bands such as Jake Hooker and the Outsiders and Jody Nix and the Texas Cowboys. "People can sit and enjoy the music, or they can get up and dance," Miers added. "You meet a lot of good people and friends you can have for a lifetime. It's also a good way for people to see one another each year … We're just trying to keep the music alive."[18]

CHAPTER THREE

Sin and *Sorrow*

After working long hours at a tough job, many people who happened to live in big cities in the mid-1900s went to honky-tonks to relax. These small bars were designed for everyone who just needed a place to go and have a little fun. Some had dance floors and live bands performing, while others relied on jukeboxes and customers with endless stacks of nickels. All of them were full of people who were tired and ready to hear music that vocalized their frustrations and their homesickness. Fame and fortune followed any band or performer that could sing about the sins and sorrows these audiences wanted to hear most.

Honky-Tonk Atmosphere

Most honky-tonks were hastily constructed buildings found on long, lonely southwestern highways. They were often a few miles outside of town, sometimes near bad or dangerous neighborhoods. The people living in more respectable neighborhoods would not tolerate the rowdy people who gathered at these establishments.

In Texas and Oklahoma, the honky-tonk clientele was mostly made up of single young men who had flocked to cities where oil was discovered—and moved on when the wells ran dry. After working grueling 12-hour shifts, these oil field workers slept in hotels, in tents, on truck beds, and even under pool tables in honky-tonks. When Saturday night came, the crowd generally became quite rowdy and ended up fighting with fists, knives, and occasionally guns. For this reason, honky-tonks were sometimes called blood buckets. Singer Floyd Tillman remembered playing some of the rougher Texas honky-tonks, "where you had to dodge [thrown] beer bottles, and when the fights broke out you were supposed to speed it up and play the music real fast."[19] Al Dexter was familiar with the honky-tonk world— the songwriter owned the Round-Up Club in Turnertown, Texas.

A harsh day of working at oil wells such as this one often sent workers in search of music and relaxation at places such as honky-tonks.

However, in 1936, when his songwriting partner James B. Paris suggested they pen a tune using the word honky-tonk, Dexter claimed he was unfamiliar with the phrase. As Dexter told music journalist Nick Tosches, "One day I went to see [James] Paris, and he said, 'I thought of a title last night that'll set the woods on fire.' I asked him what it was, and he said, 'Honky Tonk Blues.' I asked him where he got that idea … He said, 'Use your thinker-upper [brain] and let's write a song like that.'"[20]

Apparently Paris had given Dexter a good idea because the song "Honky Tonk Blues" helped define the music style that would remain popular well into the 21st century. While Dexter sings about honky-tonk lifestyle, two electric guitars create a catchy, aggressive rhythm. The lead guitar break combines hot single-note picking over jazz chords. Unlike the acoustic instruments of old-time music, the recorded sounds of the electric bass and amplified guitars were perfect for cutting through the noisy rooms of the boisterous honky-tonks, and "Honky Tonk Blues" was a major hit. Within a few years, even loyal music traditionalists, including Roy Acuff,

Ernest Tubb was a popular honky-tonk star.

were performing numbers such as "Honky Tonk Mamas."

One of the biggest honky-tonk stars of the 1940s, Ernest Tubb, was born in 1914 in Crisp, Texas. During the early part of his career, Tubb imitated Jimmie Rodgers's songs about Texas, railroad trains, and the homesick blues that inspired a later generation of honky-tonkers. When Rodgers died, Tubb was only 19 years old. He befriended Carrie, Rodgers's widow. She liked Tubb's style and loaned the lanky singer Rodgers's suit coat and his sweet-sounding Martin guitar. Tubb's early imitations of Rodgers did not sell, but the singer owned his own honky-tonk, the E&E Tavern. He commonly heard honky-tonk music playing on the tavern's jukebox but felt most of it had no heart or soul. In response, Tubb decided to create his own style, based on all he had learned from Rodgers. As Tosches explained,

> If Rodgers had taught [Tubb] anything, it was that music without power—be it the power of meanness, the power of love, the power of sentimentality, the power of sadness or madness, sweetness or venom—was music without worth. Ernest Tubb was on his way to empowering country music and recasting honky-tonk with his own new-found voice, a voice that was the sum of all he had learned from the master, and from himself. And he was on his way to glory.[21]

In 1941, Tubb recorded "Walking the Floor Over You," and it became the first million-selling honky-tonk hit. The song was also the first country "crossover" hit, selling to both country and mainstream pop music audiences. Tubb, who had been struggling in the music business for years, became an overnight sensation. He performed on the stage of the *Grand Ole Opry* and appeared in a few movies. He continued to score hits with "Drivin' Nails in My Coffin" and "Let's Say Goodbye Like We Said Hello," songs now considered honky-tonk classics.

Honky-Tonk in the Military

America's fascination with honky-tonk music changed drastically when, in December 1941, the country entered World War II. Millions of men signed up to serve in the military. To keep the music alive, honky-tonk stars, including Tubb, performed on stage for military personnel through the United Service Organizations (USO) tours. These shows, held both in the United States and overseas, exposed country performers to audiences who had either ignored or scorned this style of music before, and they created new fans.

On the home front, honky-tonk continued to top the record charts. In 1942, Al Dexter scored a crossover hit with "Pistol Packin' Mama." The song was on jukeboxes all over the country and was covered by Bing Crosby and Frank Sinatra, the biggest pop music stars at that time.

During the war, much of California's population was made up of tens of thousands of Southerners who had moved west to work in the defense industry. In the San Francisco Bay Area, as well as in Los Angeles and San Diego, nearly one-third of the newcomers were from Arkansas, Louisiana, Texas, and Oklahoma. To cater to these displaced Southerners, roadside honky-tonks opened near defense plants and military bases. Radio programmers saw gold in honky-tonk, so nearly every major California station featured barn dance shows and honky-tonk music acts.

With country breaking into the mainstream, it was inevitable that performers' clothing would become more glamorous. A Russian tailor named Nutya Kotlyrenko, known professionally as Nudie Cohn, opened a shop in his Los Angeles garage and sewed fake diamonds, called rhinestones, onto western suits. These suits with rhinestone decorations were called Nudie suits. By the end of the decade, Cohn had moved to Hollywood, and nearly every honky-tonk singer who could afford it had a shimmering Nudie suit in the closet.

With guitar playing as flashy as a Nudie suit, Merle Travis became one of the West Coast's hottest guitar slingers. Born in Kentucky, his songs, such as "Sixteen Tons" and "Dark as a Dungeon," are odes to the suffering faced by coal miners. Travis also wrote humorous songs such as "Smoke! Smoke! Smoke! (That Cigarette)" and "Divorce Me C.O.D." Travis was known for his unique thumb-picking guitar style, now known as Travis picking, in which the thumb plays a steady rhythm of bass notes while the first and second fingers tickle out the melody on the higher strings.

The Unique Sound of Hank Williams

While the honky-tonkers were pioneering their own sound in California, singer-songwriter Hank Williams was making a name for himself appearing on barn dance radio shows and touring honky-tonk bars in his native Alabama. Williams was born in rural Butler County in 1923. As a young boy, he learned to play music from an African American street musician named Rufus "Tee-Tot" Payne. By the time he was 18, Williams was performing his own songs on local radio stations, and he had his own band.

Williams had a natural singing style like Ernest Tubb, but he also had a unique sound to his voice, based on the vocal wail perfected by Acuff. Honky-tonk fans loved it. Williams was signed in 1946 by the Nashville music publishing company founded by Acuff and Fred Rose, a successful songwriter. Like other music publishers, Acuff-Rose signed composers to write hit songs, picked artists to record the tunes, promoted the music, and collected a percentage of the profits—called royalties—from sales of the recordings.

Nudie suits grabbed the audience's attention as they reflected the bright stage lights.

As a young man, Hank Williams played his music on the sidewalks of Montgomery, Alabama.

Acuff-Rose selected the best songs for Williams, created musical arrangements, booked recording sessions, and hired musicians. This system, called artists and repertoire, or A&R, was created to oversee the artistic development of a recording talent. It was first used for Williams, but A&R would eventually become standard throughout the music industry.

When Williams was signed by Acuff-Rose, he was only 23. The pain and torment he sang about in his songs came, in large part, from his personal life. He drank alcohol a lot and suffered from depression. He deeply loved his wife, Audrey Mae Sheppard, but his drinking caused marital problems. As Wolff wrote,

Hank first met … Sheppard while he was touring with a medicine show in southern Alabama. A year later they were married, and almost just as quickly the arguing began, usually fueled by Hank's appetite for booze. Drinking was a habit that would land Hank in jail, dry-docked in a sanatorium, and face down in the gutter many times over … And neither Audrey, nor Hank's mother Lillie, could keep him sober when beer was on his mind.[22]

In 1949, Williams went to Nashville and recorded "Lovesick Blues," a song that perfectly mirrored his troubled relationship with his wife. The song was Williams's first big hit. It stayed on the country charts for 16 weeks, earning the singer a spot on the *Grand Ole Opry*.

While it was his drinking that was causing much of the problems with Audrey, Williams portrayed himself as a victim. Using his stormy life for songwriting material, he penned a string of classic songs, including "Cold Cold Heart," "You Win Again," "I'm So Lonesome I Could Cry," and "Your Cheatin' Heart." These songs were hits on the country charts and were later recorded by pop artists. All the fame and fortune these successes brought Williams meant little to him, however, as he sank into deep depression after Audrey left him. In the early 1950s, Williams was in terrible shape. He was drinking more than ever, missing his wife (despite whatever he sang in his songs), and experimenting with drugs. Around this time, he wrote another depressing song: "I'll Never Get Out of This World Alive."

In October 1952, while still technically married to Audrey, Williams married another woman. While they had a marriage ceremony in front of a Justice of the Peace, they also held another marriage ceremony at the New Orleans Civic Auditorium, in front of 14,000 fans. However, Williams's life was tragically cut short not long after this wedding. On January 1, 1953,

Williams died in the back of a Cadillac on the way to a concert in Canton, Ohio. His official cause of death was heart failure. Although he was only 29 years old, Williams had recorded more than 200 songs during his 6-year career.

Stars who die tragically at the height of their careers often become legends, and Williams is no exception. His rise to fame and tragic end was told in the 2016 movie *I Saw the Light*, starring Tom Hiddleston as Hank Williams and Elizabeth Olsen as Audrey. Additionally, his personal, introspective songs permanently changed the sound of country and paved the way for a new generation of honky-tonk singers that included Lefty Frizzell, Webb Pierce, Ray Price, Faron Young, Hank Snow, and George Jones.

A Singing Angel

Although honky-tonk music had largely belonged to male singers for more than a decade, that changed in summer 1952. Tennessee native Kitty Wells rose to the top of the charts with "It Wasn't God Who Made Honky Tonk Angels." Wells started her career singing backup vocals for her husband, a struggling country artist named Johnnie Wright. At the age of 33, she was about to retire from the music business to be a full-time mother, but a record producer persuaded her to record "It Wasn't God Who Made Honky Tonk Angels."

Kitty Wells was one of the most popular country artists in the mid-1950s.

The song was written in response to the line from honky-tonk star Hank Thompson's song "The Wild Side of Life," in which he sang, "I didn't know God made honky-tonk angels / I might have known you'd never make a wife." In her song, Wells responded: "It wasn't God who made honky-tonk angels / As you said in the words of your song / Too many times married men think they're still single / That has caused many a good girl to go wrong."[23]

"It Wasn't God Who Made Honky Tonk Angels" shot to number 1 and stayed there for six weeks.

Wells went on to record more than a dozen hits in the 1950s and early 1960s, earning her the title of Queen of Country Music. After "It Wasn't God Who Made Honky Tonk Angels" became a hit, Nashville producers wanted to find another female vocalist who could match Kitty Wells's success. They found one in Patsy Cline, a hard-drinking, rowdy musician who started her singing career at the age of 16, performing in honky-tonks.

Cline's first success came in 1957 after she sang "Walkin' After Midnight" on the popular television show *Arthur Godfrey's Talent Scouts*—similar to today's *American Idol* and *The Voice*. In 1961, Cline's "I Fall to Pieces" went to number 1 on the country charts and crossed over to the pop charts, rising to number 12. Cline's singing could grab the attention of any listener. Critics immediately recognized how powerful, versatile, and unique her voice was. She was capable of singing in countless styles, all effortlessly. Tragically, on March 5, 1963, when Cline was coming home from a concert, her private plane crashed due to bad weather in Tennessee. Although she was only performing for a few years, Cline's singing style has continued to influence countless female country, pop, and rock vocalists.

Although Cline, Williams, and Wells are well recognized and respected honky-tonk heroes, they were not the only ones who helped make the distinct sound of honky-tonk a lasting style. Years later, honky-tonk is still a well-loved music style within country music. Chances are that as long as there are hearts to get broken, lonesome highways to explore, and honky-tonk bars to step inside, the music will go on.

CHAPTER FOUR

The National
Music Throne of Nashville

Country music was in trouble during the mid-to-late 1950s. Most of the radios, record players, and jukeboxes were blasting out top rock and roll tunes. Fiddles faded and steel guitars grew quiet, replaced by drums and electric guitars. No one was sure if country music could be saved. They believed the best solution was merging styles and asking a few talented performers to create records that both country music fans and rock fans would enjoy.

Rough voices were out, and smooth, velvety voices were in. String sections took over for steel guitars. Elvis Presley recorded "Don't Be Cruel," and songs by southern rockers Jerry Lee Lewis, Gene Vincent, and Buddy Holly straddled the line of rock and country, drawing in new teenage fans. This sentiment was on display in a 1957 article in the music industry magazine *Music Reporter*. Editor Charlie Lamb wrote that Nashville "reigned supreme 'on the national music throne by virtue of the undisputed dominance of rockabilly music, produced by one-time country singers to whom the style comes as naturally as breathing.'"[24]

Although Lamb was correct, the solution was not made to last. Elvis, Gene, and Jerry Lee were a disaster for country music. When Nashville producers tried to cater to the tastes of teenagers with rock music, they ignored the traditional country audience, which was largely white, working-class, and middle-aged. While alienating their traditional audience, Nashville producers led millions of southern teenagers to abandon country music. Many of these young adults felt the music had nothing new to say to them. Country music's sales plummeted.

The dramatic impact of rock was painfully obvious at the Ryman Auditorium, where the *Grand Ole Opry* was held every Saturday night from 1943 until 1974. From the mid-1920s until 1954, the show was sold out nearly every weekend. By 1958, the auditorium was often more than half empty at show time. The energetic live shows put on by massive rock and roll acts, including Elvis, were simply not being matched by any country acts at the time. As such, people could simply not go back to the relatively tame country sound.

As America's music tastes changed, there was a ripple effect. In 1957, the *Grand Ole Opry* radio show was pulling in fewer and fewer listeners. In 1960, Chicago's WLS dropped *National Barn Dance*. Both programs were forced to struggle along on local stations. These changes, in turn, impacted country music sales. After World War II, as the number of radio stations grew nationwide, station managers implemented a new concept called "top 40." Rather than play music to fit local tastes, programmers picked 40 top-selling records and played them repeatedly. By the late 1950s, rock and roll dominated top-40 radio. This caused hundreds of country stations to switch over to the same format. In 1961, there were only 81 full-time country stations left in the United States, down from 650 in 1949. This was due, in large part, to the fact that by 1955, more than half of the homes in the country had a television. Radios were largely abandoned in favor of the new medium. It was a hard time for the country music industry, and musicians and executives were desperate to regain their former fortunes.

The Modern Nashville Sound

In 1958, country music executives formed the Country Music Association (CMA) to promote the financial interests of their industry. They focused on getting more country radio stations on the air and convincing advertisers that the millions of white, middle-aged country music fans were an important segment of the buying public.

The old-time, bluegrass, and honky-tonk that had made earlier country music so successful was out, they reassured advertisers, and had been thoroughly replaced. A CMA consultant issued a memo stating: "Modern country music has no relationship to rural or mountain life. It is the music of this *Nation*, of this country, the music of the people. You find no screech fiddles, no twangy guitars, no mournful nasal twangs in the *modern* Nashville sound of country music."[25]

While the CMA promoted country music, record producers, such as Owen Bradley, Don Law, and guitar virtuoso Chet Atkins, worked to rid country of "screech fiddles" and "twangy guitars." Steel guitars, fiddle breaks, and nasal vocals were muted. The new style featured smooth country crooners backed by gospel-like choruses and lush string arrangements provided by the Nashville Symphony Orchestra. The sounds were relaxed. The beat was easygoing, and the feel was the exact opposite of the jittery noise made by rock and rollers.

The new brand of country music was called everything from country pop to countrypolitan, or, simply, the Nashville sound. Most lyrics were written by a few proven songwriters. Husband-and-wife team Felice and Boudleaux Bryant wrote chart toppers such as "Love Hurts" and "Richest Man in the World" in addition to the Everly Brothers' hits "Bye Bye Love" and "Wake Up Little Susie." Cindy Walker penned "You Don't Know Me," sung by Eddy Arnold, and "Distant Drums," which was a hit for Jim Reeves. Harlan Howard composed "I Fall to Pieces," made famous by Patsy Cline, and "I've Got a Tiger by the Tail," a chart topper for Buck Owens, the king of the Bakersfield, California, country sound. At countrypolitan recording sessions, instrumentation was supplied by an exclusive group of talented session musicians. They appeared, often without credit, on thousands of records. The basic countrypolitan

Buck Owens was a frequent visitor to television programs such as The Jimmy Dean Show.

THE BAKERSFIELD SOUND

In the early 1960s, a new sound emerged in Bakersfield, California, that was meant to challenge Nashville's countrypolitan sound. The Bakersfield sound was notable for its twangy picking style on the guitar, rock rhythms, and gliding pedal steel licks. The king of the Bakersfield sound was the Texas-born Buck Owens. In 1956, Owens made his first record for Capitol Records in Los Angeles with his band, the Buckaroos. Rather than play the honky-tonk style popularized by Hank Williams, Owens ripped it up with fast rock rhythms, backed by lead player Don Rich on his electric Fender Telecaster guitar. Owens had a string of hits beginning with 1963's "Act Naturally," which was later covered by the Beatles. After that breakthrough, Owens compiled 20 top hits on the country charts before 1972.

Although he achieved international fame, Owens refused to abandon Bakersfield, which was soon nicknamed Buckersfield in his honor. In 1996, Owens turned his adopted hometown into a tourist attraction, opening the Buck Owens Crystal Palace, a $7 million museum, concert hall, and restaurant. It continues to draw people today to watch music performances, see life-size statues of rock and country stars, and marvel at Owens's 1972 Pontiac convertible, complete with steer horns mounted on the hood, hung over the palace's bar. Although he died in 2006, Buck Owens and the Bakersfield sound continue to influence country music well into the 2010s.

session band of the 1960s consisted of Grady Martin on guitar, Roy Madison Huskey Jr. (known as Junior Huskey) on bass, Floyd Cramer or Hargus "Pig" Robbins on piano, Charlie McCoy on harmonica, and Buddy Harmon on drums. Background vocals on countless Nashville recordings were provided by the Anita Kerr Singers. In addition to leading her vocal group, Kerr provided arrangements on many recordings. She was also one of the only women hired to produce for RCA Records in the 1960s.

Gibson and Reeves

The biggest stars of the Nashville sound were the singers, and it was their faces and names highlighted on the record covers. The first official countrypolitan hits were Don Gibson's 1958 "Oh Lonesome Me" and "I Can't Stop Loving You," both produced by Chet Atkins. Both of these mournful songs were written by the singer on the same day. Gibson was known as the Sad Poet because he wrote so many hits about heartbreak and loneliness—but his clear, melodious singing voice came to define country crooners of the era.

"Gentleman" Jim Reeves was another velvet-voiced singer who embodied the Nashville sound.

Born in Texas in 1923, Reeves began his career in 1952, filling in for Hank Williams when the honky-tonk superstar was drunk and failed to appear on *Louisiana Hayride*. In 1959, Reeves scored a major hit with "He'll Have to Go." During the early 1960s, Reeves dominated the country charts with slow, gospel-tinged songs such as "Guilty" and "Welcome to My World." Reeves loved to fly his own airplane to gigs; when his small plane crashed in 1964, the beloved singer was killed instantly. He was inducted into the Country Music Hall of Fame in 1967.

Parton and Wagoner

Porter Wagoner, born in 1927 in the Ozark Mountains, was known as the Thin Man from West Plains (Missouri). Wagoner began his career singing in honky-tonks. His flamboyant style included blond hair styled in an inflated pompadour and outrageous, shimmering Nudie suits.

Wagoner's first number-1 hit, "A Satisfied Mind," made him a national star in 1955. By 1957, he was a regular at the *Grand Ole Opry*. Throughout his career, Wagoner mixed the honky-tonk style with the Nashville sound, making sure the strings and choruses did not dilute the true country edge. The lyrics of his hit songs—such as "I've Enjoyed as Much of This as I Can Stand," "Cold Dark Waters," "Green, Green Grass of Home," and "The Cold Hard Facts of Life"—demonstrated the sentimentality often found in country pop.

The flashy singer achieved national acclaim in 1960 with his own television program, *The Porter Wagoner Show*, which featured corny jokes and country music. Wagoner's backup singers were Norma Jean Beasler and Dolly Parton, both of whom became stars in their own right. Beasler had 13 country singles between 1963 and 1968. Parton and Wagoner went on to record several best-selling albums together and had a string of number-1 hits between 1967 and 1973.

Upon embarking on a solo career, one of Parton's first songs as a solo artist was the famous hit "I Will Always Love You," which was later covered by Whitney Houston. Right from the start of her solo career, Parton was quickly recognized for her songwriting talents, singing ability, and sharp business sense.

Parton, born in 1946, has true country roots. Her early life reads like lyrics from an old song. She was the fourth of twelve children born to a poverty-stricken couple in a cabin in the Smoky Mountains of Tennessee. Like so many others, she was inspired by the music she heard in church and the songs she sang with her family. When she was 14, Parton's uncle took her to

*Dolly Parton and Porter Wagoner often performed together.
Their duets are considered country music classics.*

Nashville, where she recorded an original song titled "Puppy Love." By the time she graduated high school in 1964, she was writing hit songs for other artists.

In 1967, Parton began writing songs demonstrating a strong, feminist point of view. Wolff described the ironically titled song "Dumb Blonde" as "a take-no-punches song about smashing sexist stereotypes. Like other songs soon to come ('Just Because I'm a Woman' [and] 'When Possession Gets Too Strong') … it revealed a young woman unafraid to put forward a strong female perspective."[26]

Parton also painted a realistic picture of her poverty-stricken childhood and the hardships she overcame in songs such as "Coat of Many Colors," "To Daddy," and "In the Good Old Days (When Times Were Bad)." By the late 1970s, Parton had transcended the role of country music singer to become a movie star and a superstar with a broad, mainstream fan base. In 1986, she opened a theme park called

Dollywood. The park attracted more than 1 million visitors the first year, and by 2017, average yearly attendance was more than triple that number.

In the 2010s, Parton's popularity has still not faded. In 2018, Netflix announced that a new series—based on some of Parton's classic songs—would premiere in 2019. Parton herself is set to appear in some episodes, making it a must-watch program for fans of the country music classics.

Honesty and Controversy

Loretta Lynn is another country singer who used autobiographical material to write hit songs. Lynn's life was one of struggle and hardship followed by fame and fortune. She was born in 1932 in isolated Butcher Hollow, Kentucky. Her father struggled to provide for his family, laboring for little pay in the local coal mines. Loretta was around 16 when she married Oliver Lynn Jr. By the time she was 20, her family had grown to include four children. Additionally, by the time Loretta was 34, she was also a grandmother.

Despite this busy family life and a sometimes stormy marriage, Lynn aspired to become a singing star. In 1960, she recorded her first single: "I'm a Honky Tonk Girl," which launched her career. Lynn touched the hearts of average country men and women with songs about her life and the world around her. She wrote about honky-tonks, coal mines, drunk people, cheating husbands, and backstabbing women. Songs such as "Who's Gonna Take the Garbage Out," and "Your Squaw Is on the Warpath" sum up the rough and tough attitudes of this country star. In a segment of the music industry aimed at a largely conservative country audience, Lynn often created controversy with her honest subject matter. Some of her songs were even banned from country radio. For example, "Dear Uncle Sam," released in 1966 at the height of the Vietnam War, was written from the perspective of a wife whose husband was a soldier killed in the war.

Despite her coverage of what were considered controversial or hot-button topics at the time, Lynn's honesty, clear vocals, and strong songwriting kept her at the top of the charts. In 1970, she had a number-1 hit with the autobiographical "Coal Miner's Daughter," which was also the title of her 1976 autobiography and the movie based on it that was released in 1980. Lynn was inducted into the Country Music Hall of Fame in 1988, and since then, she has continued to record and perform. In 2016, at the age of 84, she released the album *Full Circle*.

Lynn and Parton were part of a group of high-spirited, groundbreaking women who

*Loretta Lynn attracted listeners with her sharp,
honest lyrics and her fearless approach to songwriting.*

were recording in Nashville in the 1960s. Other female performers, including Skeeter Davis, Dottie West, Connie Smith, and Jeannie C. Riley, wrote songs of sass, spirit, and sentimentality that provided inspiration to countless women who grew up listening to their music.

Unexpected Hits

By 1964, country music fans were hungry for different types of songs. Singer-songwriter Roger Miller was a Nashville veteran who was there to provide some novelty and fun. Miller had been in Nashville for years, struggling to get his songs in front of producers and country singers. In the early 1960s, he had a few minor hits recorded by George Jones and Faron Young, but money was scarce. In desperation, Miller decided to record some of his novelty songs himself, borrowing more than $1,000 to buy studio time.

Miller wrote one of those recorded songs, "Dang Me," in just a few minutes in a Phoenix, Arizona, hotel room. He was shocked when the song went to number 1 on the country charts in 1964, crossing over to the pop charts soon after. Miller followed that surprising accomplishment with the hit singles "Chug-a-Lug," "Do Wacka-Do," and his anthem (a song that speaks to a mass group of people) "King of the Road," which was released in 1965. In 1964, "Dang Me" netted Miller five Grammy Awards, with six more the following year for "King of the Road" and his album *The Return of Roger Miller*.

Miller's success came at a time when the Beatles were dominating the record charts, along with the Animals, the Rolling Stones, and

HISTORY AND ADVENTURE

In the late 1950s, a revival of interest in folk music on college campuses provided a market for a new type of country music based on the old-time historical ballads. Known as sagas or epic music, these songs combined up-tempo beats and slick arrangements with adventure stories that could have been taken from popular novels.

In 1959, Johnny Horton released the first of these hits with "The Battle of New Orleans." He followed it up with several crossover epic hits, including "North to Alaska," "Sink the Bismarck," and "When It's Springtime in Alaska," before his premature death in a 1960 car accident.

Horton's success inspired Marty Robbins to write "El Paso." This 10-verse number centers on a cowboy who shoots a rival in a Texas bar because he made a pass at a beautiful dancer. Robbins went on to record a number of cowboy and gunfighter ballads popular throughout the 1960s, including "Big Iron" and "The Little Green Valley." Other notable Nashville ballads include Jimmy Dean's "Big Bad John," Jim Reeves's "The Blizzard," and Eddy Arnold's "Tennessee Stud."

the Kinks. Even during the pop music era known as the British Invasion, Miller held his own with both country and college crowds. Whoever heard Miller's songs seemed to love his wickedly clever lyrics, tightly honed arrangements, and wacky

CONFLICTS IN COUNTRY

In the late 1960s, the United States was a divided country. Millions of young people rallied in the streets to protest the war in Vietnam, while much of the older generation supported the conflict. During this era, rock radio stations were filled with antiwar songs such as "Eve of Destruction" by Barry McGuire, "Give Peace a Chance" by John Lennon, and "Unknown Soldier" by the Doors. In response to this · musical outpouring, largely conservative country singers and songwriters in Nashville fired back with their own songs supporting the war while condemning the protesters.

The most famous of these anthems, "Okie From Muskogee," was released by Merle Haggard in 1969, one of the most divisive years of a conflict-ridden decade. Haggard wrote the song after he became disheartened while watching anti-Vietnam War protests on television. The song, which made Haggard a national

MERLE HAGGARD

Capitol®

Merle Haggard did not agree with the protests of the Vietnam War that were frequent in the 1960s, and his music reflected his beliefs.

star, argued to listeners that in Muskogee, Oklahoma, no one smokes marijuana or wears their hair long, and they proudly wave the country's flag. Other hit songs protesting the protesters included Dave Dudley's "What We're Fighting For" and Ernest Tubb's "It's America (Love It or Leave It)."

sense of humor.

Miller was far from the only Nashville singer to ride to the top of the charts with novelty songs. In the mid-1960s, Dave Dudley—a former semiprofessional baseball player—combined two things country fans loved: big trucks and hard-driving tunes. His songs were wildly popular with country audiences. Dudley's most famous tune, "Six Days on the Road," was a million-selling truck-driving anthem covered by everyone from blues artist Taj Mahal to country rockers the Flying Burrito Brothers. A sampling of Dudley's titles, including "There Ain't No Easy Run" and "Trucker's Prayer" reflect the serious and the humorous aspects of propelling an 18-wheeler down the road. Dudley sang many of his amusing lyrics with mumbles and slurs, leading some to suspect he was intoxicated when he was recording. Intoxicated or not, his music kept people interested.

Welcome to Music City, U.S.A.

In the decades since Nashville was given the nickname Music City, U.S.A., it has only continued to expand and evolve. The creation of the CMA has supported Nashville's

fame. In 1965, there were more than 200 radio stations devoted to playing country music. As of 2018, that number has skyrocketed, hitting more than 2,000 stations, officially making it the most popular radio format in the country. In 1967, the Country Music Hall of Fame opened, followed by the formation of the Country Music Awards, a huge event that continues today. In 1983, Country Music Television (CMT) added to the lineup of music resources for country's millions of fans.

Today, Nashville's Ryman Auditorium still draws people from all over the world to see amazing concerts and stroll past memorabilia from famous artists. Thousands of hopeful singers, songwriters, and musicians come there to walk the famous Music Row, where all the major record labels have offices and studios. During the annual Tin Pan South Songwriters Festival, hundreds of optimistic men and women perform at many of the more than 180 music venues throughout Nashville. From the first notes played on the *Grand Ole Opry*'s opening night to the thriving hub of music and fame it is today, Nashville is the true heart of country music.

CHAPTER FIVE

Music City and
the Counterculture

While there is little question that Nashville was becoming the country music capital of the world, there was also little question that the city promoted conservative political and religious values. Many of Nashville's residents were completely puzzled and even outraged by the values and behaviors in other parts of the country. It was the mid-1960s, and millions of young people were experimenting with drugs, wearing long hair, developing their own slang, and wearing everything from tie-dyed shirts and jeans to sandals and love beads (a necklace made of small beads to symbolize peace). Known largely as the hippie movement or counterculture, its followers rejected traditional beliefs about politics, romance, and religion—and the many conservatives in Nashville did not like that. However, there were some country artists whose careers reflected various aspects of the rebellious spirit of this period of time.

The Man in Black

Johnny Cash is recognized today as a towering legend of country music. Born in Kingsland, Arkansas, in 1932, he began singing and playing guitar as a young boy. Despite his interest in music from youth, he went on to serve in the military—stationed in Germany—until the early 1950s. Almost immediately after returning to the United States, however, he joined the Tennessee Two and caught the attention of Sam Phillips, an executive for Sun Records. Cash was signed to Sun in 1955, and in 1956, Cash had a number-1 hit with his first single for the company: "I Walk the Line." Even after decades of number-1 hits and major successes, "I Walk the Line" remains one of Cash's most beloved songs. By the late 1950s, Cash was a huge star all across the United States, but his grueling touring schedule had him playing hundreds of shows every year. Despite becoming the top-selling country musician during this time, Cash was drinking heavily and taking a large number of drugs. After receiving an overwhelmingly positive critical and commercial response to "Ring of Fire" in 1963, Cash's life spun out of control due to his substance abuse.

Though Cash had always been sympathetic to prison inmates and those who suffered under the law, he did not have any real history of being incarcerated. He had been arrested several times and spent several nights in jails and holding cells, but he was not a career criminal. In 1965, however, he was arrested in El Paso, Texas, for smuggling drugs across the border with Mexico and was banned from the *Grand Ole Opry*. Though he only paid a small fine for this crime, his highly conservative audience had started turning against him. Though the "bad boy" image of drug use and a criminal lifestyle might have appealed to America's rebellious youth, Cash's core audience was largely against drugs and certainly did not support their favorite performer's struggles with the law. With declining popularity and increased substance abuse, Cash's marriage suffered; in 1966, he was divorced.

In 1967, with the help of his future wife June Carter, Cash sobered up. Cash and Carter had been working closely together since 1961, singing a number of duets that showcased their strong country voices.

Around the time of their marriage in 1968, they sang several popular country duets, including "Jackson" and "It Ain't Me, Babe," that helped get Cash's life back on track. After examining his lifestyle and choices, Cash began to distance himself from his previous professional image. He had been known as the Man in Black because of his habit of wearing all black clothing (which was seen as very edgy and unique), and the attitude that went along with that persona had helped him sell records in his early career. However, after his struggles with alcohol, drugs, and the law, Cash wanted to partially turn over a new leaf.

After achieving sobriety and cleaning up his act, Cash had a major comeback after releasing the iconic concert album *At Folsom Prison*. In 1969, Cash had his biggest hit yet with "A Boy Named Sue." This song was written by Shel Silverstein, the famous poet and author also responsible for writing *Where the Sidewalk Ends* and *The Giving Tree*. Though the worlds of country music and children's literature rarely come together, Cash and Silverstein's humorous song was an enormous success. The same year "A Boy Named Sue" was sweeping the country, Cash created a variety television program titled *The Johnny Cash Show*, which ran for two years on ABC. Guests on this show included Bob Dylan and Ray Charles, both

Johnny Cash—the Man in Black—is shown here performing at a concert in the 1980s.

of whom were major musical talents in their own right.

Following the turnaround of his life in the 1970s, Cash felt the pull of his Christian background. He was officially ordained as a minister after obtaining a degree in theology, and parts of his later career are marked by his performance of gospel songs. Though largely remembered for his work in country music, his gospel songs were also highly successful, and he brought a new, refreshing attitude to the genre.

In 1980, the legendary, influential perfomer was inducted into the Country Music Hall of Fame. Cash also was inducted into the Rock and Roll Hall of Fame in 1992 because so many of his popular songs could be considered crossover smash hits. Shortly before his death in 2003 at the age of 71, he even recorded a powerful cover of rock band

Nine Inch Nails' song "Hurt," which resonated with music fans. In 2005, the movie *Walk the Line* about Cash's life was released, with Joaquin Phoenix as Cash and Reese Witherspoon as June Carter. The album *American V: A Hundred Highways* was released in 2006, and it included the last two songs he wrote before passing away: "I Came to Believe" and "Like the 309." Cash's impact on music is still felt today—in 2017, the annual Johnny Cash Heritage Festival was started in Cash's boyhood home in Arkansas to celebrate his impact on music.

Bob Dylan's Country Sounds

When singer Joni Mitchell visited Nashville in the late 1960s, accompanied by an entourage of West Coast male musicians, she recalled "everybody was hostile to them. People yelled, called them shaggy-hairs and hippies. They felt unsafe."[27] The hippies, in turn, nicknamed the country music fans rednecks, a derogatory term replacing the term hillbilly by the 1960s.

Given this type of hostile environment, people were surprised when Bob Dylan released the album *John Wesley Harding* in 1967.

Bob Dylan (right) had long been known mainly for his protest songs, often sung as duets with Joan Baez (left), until he took more of a country-inspired approach.

Recorded in Nashville, the album combined Dylan's trademark storytelling lyrics with simple country music. By this time, Dylan was one of the most famous singers in the world. He achieved fame in 1963 for protest songs about issues such as racial inequality, nuclear fallout, and the bomb builders he called masters of war. In 1964, Dylan abandoned political songs for long epics. Today, these influential songs from the mid-1960s, such as "Mr. Tambourine Man," "Gates of Eden," "Just Like a Woman," "Visions Of Johanna," and "Like a Rolling Stone," are considered timeless classics. In 1969, Dylan followed up *John Wesley Harding* with *Nashville Skyline*. It was a mix of honky-tonk piano, pedal steel guitar, Dobro, and drums. The new album included songs that sounded a great deal like Hank Williams's songs. It also included "Girl From the North Country," which was a duet with country music legend Johnny Cash. The single from the album, "Lay Lady Lay," with its pedal steel guitar and catchy rhythm track played on bongos and a cowbell, was Dylan's biggest hit to date. By the summer of 1969, *Nashville Skyline* was the best-selling album in the United States, and Dylan had been credited for inventing a new musical style called country rock.

Dylan's music made him a hero of the counterculture movement, but his roots were in country music. When he first heard Hank Williams on the *Grand Ole Opry* radio show, Dylan was about 10 years old. As he wrote in his 2004 autobiography, "The first time I heard Hank … the sound of his voice went through me like an electric rod and I managed to get a hold of a few of his [records] … and I played them endlessly."[28]

With and Without Parsons

The Byrds were a group that topped the charts in 1965 by covering several Dylan songs. Less than a year before 1969's *Nashville Skyline*, they released *Sweetheart of the Rodeo*. By 1967, the group had evolved into a psychedelic rock band with the hit "Eight Miles High." The song was banned on many radio stations for its alleged drug references. In 1968, the Byrds released the album *The Notorious Byrd Brothers*. The record mixed excessive psychedelic studio noise with folk, country, and jazz—sometimes within a single song.

Their career faltering, the Byrds invited 22-year-old Gram Parsons to join the group. Parsons was a Georgia native who was strongly influenced by Merle Haggard and George Jones. With Parsons at the helm, the Byrds created *Sweetheart of the Rodeo*. Recorded in Nashville, the album features banjo, pedal steel, and mandolin playing authentic bluegrass and honky-tonk. On the album, the Byrds played several country standards, a few Dylan songs, and Parsons's original country rock songs "Hickory Wind" and "One Hundred Years from Now."

Despite its groundbreaking sound, *Sweetheart of the Rodeo* was not well received. The album only reached number 77 on the Billboard Top Albums chart. A review in *Rolling Stone* gave the effort faint praise: "The new Byrds do not sound like Buck Owens … They aren't that good. The material they've chosen to record, or rather, the way they perform the material, is simple, relaxed and folky. It's not pretentious, it's pretty … It ought to make the 'Easy-Listening' charts."[29]

Due to conflict with other band members, Gram Parsons left the Byrds soon after *Sweetheart of the Rodeo* was released. He quickly formed a new band called the Flying Burrito Brothers with bassist Chris Ethridge, pedal steel guitar player "Sneaky" Pete Kleinow, and the Byrds' former bassist and mandolin player Chris Hillman. In 1969, the pioneering Flying Burrito Brothers' debut album *Gilded Palace of Sin* was released. Parsons, working with Hillman and Ethridge, wrote the majority of songs on the album.

The cover of *Gilded Palace of Sin* shows the four band members dressed in gaudy Nudie suits, but the group's intention to break

tradition is obvious from their custom-made outfits. Parsons's suit is adorned with images of marijuana leaves, along with pills and capsules assumed to be LSD, amphetamines, and barbiturates. While many country artists, including Johnny Cash and George Jones, were addicted to drugs in the 1960s, the public was largely unaware of this fact. The Flying Burrito Brothers seemed to be flaunting their drug use and, for the first time, connecting country music to recreational drugs promoted by the counterculture.

Gilded Palace of Sin only sold around 60,000 copies upon its release. After recording a second album, Parsons left the group. *Gilded Palace of Sin* is considered one of the most influential country rock albums. Keith Richards, guitarist for the Rolling Stones, became one of Parsons's biggest fans. They spent a great deal of time together, and Parsons was a strong influence on the Stones' songs "Honky Tonk Woman," "Dead Flowers," "Sweet Virginia," and "Wild Horses."

During the early 1970s, Parsons released two solo albums, one of which was released the year after he died. Several songs were backed by Emmylou Harris, who was on her way to becoming a huge country star. In 1973, Parsons died from an overdose of drugs and alcohol. Long after his death, dozens of artists, including Elvis Costello, U2,

Marty Stuart, Tom Petty, and the Eagles, still credit Parsons with inspiring their music.

After Gram Parsons's death in 1973, Emmylou Harris kept his legacy alive. She toured with his old band and popularized some of his songs. In 1981, punk rocker Elvis Costello released an entire album called *Almost Blue* which consisted of covers of Hank Williams, Johnny Cash, and Gram Parsons songs. By the 1990s, Parsons had become more popular in death than he was in life. In 1993, Rhino Records issued *Commemorativo: A Tribute to Gram Parsons*, and in 1999, Harris produced the popular tribute album *Return of the Grievous Angel*, featuring Lucinda Williams, Steve Earle, the Pretenders, Beck, and Sheryl Crow.

Parsons's daughter Polly has also played a large role in continuing to popularize her father's music. Between 1996 and 2006, she produced *Gram Fest*, or the *Cosmic American Music Festival*, in Joshua Tree, California. In 2004, another Gram Parsons tribute concert, held in Santa Barbara, California, attracted Keith Richards, Norah Jones, Lucinda Williams, and other stars. Several books and films have been made about Parsons, and he has been nominated to be in the Country Music Hall of Fame three times as of 2018.

The Outlaws of Country Music

After Gram Parsons died, a genre known as outlaw country music dominated the 1970s. Keith Richards credits Parsons for paving the way for the outlaws: "Basically, you wouldn't have had Waylon Jennings, you wouldn't have had all of that outlaw movement without Gram Parsons. He showed them a new approach, that country music isn't just this narrow thing that appeals to rednecks. He did it single-handed."[30]

The leading outlaws—Jennings, Willie Nelson, David Allan Coe, and Bobby Bare—rebelled against the syrupy-sweet Nashville sound perfected in the 1960s. The outlaws wrote their own material or chose their songs to cover, plus they used their own road bands in the studio rather than playing with session musicians unfamiliar with their repertoire. These bands had a hard-edged sound, driven by loud pedal steels, twangy electric guitars, and the driving two-step country beat held down by a thumping bass.

The live-hard country sound of the outlaws appealed to both country and rock audiences. After Jennings recorded the Lee Clayton song "Ladies Love Outlaws" in 1972, the movement took off. The renegade underground quickly became mainstream. Dozens of songs displaying the outlaw

Jessi Colter and Waylon Jennings were a musical power couple who took the outlaw country world by storm.

attitude appeared on records. By 1976, the sound was so popular that *Wanted! The Outlaws* became the first country album to achieve platinum status, selling more than 1 million units. (While many songs and albums sold more than 1 million units before 1976, the Recording Industry Association of America [RIAA] did not create the platinum distinction until 1976.) It featured songs by Jennings, Tompall Glaser, and Jennings's wife at the time, Jessi Colter. Many of the songs on this album quickly became staples of 1970s country—and even rock—radio. Meanwhile, Nelson's *Red Headed Stranger*—an album that shocked record executives for its sparse, acoustic arrangements—went gold (500,000 units sold) within five months of its release.

Outlaw country dominated the charts with honest songs about the lives of the performers. Rather

THE WILDEST OUTLAW

Outlaw hits such as "Longhaired Redneck", "Willie, Waylon and Me," and "Take This Job and Shove It" were written by David Allan Coe. Though his name is not as widely renowned as some of outlaw country's other huge stars, it was Coe who truly defined the outlaw country state of mind. On his albums and in his songwriting, he was a musical genius, combining catchy rhythms with clever lyrics and an appealing sound. When he played concerts, he often wore extremely flashy clothes, a wig, and sometimes even a mask. His persona was built around his nickname (also the title of one of his albums): the Mysterious Rhinestone Cowboy. Professionally, he was regarded as a talented musician with a bright future.

It was Coe's past, however, that made him the wildest of the outlaw country performers. He had a larger-than-life personality and a mysterious background story—Coe claimed that he had been in and out of prisons, gangs, and other criminal activities from a young age. He said that his tough, hard-knock experiences added fuel to his musical fire. However, some of his claims were debunked by a *Rolling Stone* exposé, which argued that he exaggerated his criminal past and hardcore lifestyle to gather increased attention. Regardless of which aspects of Coe's life were real—and which were fake—it is no question that he was a pure symbol of the outlaw country lifestyle.

than trying to appeal to strait-laced country audiences, the outlaws sang such tunes as "Wasted Days and Wasted Nights" and "Take This Job and Shove It."

Campbell, Rogers, and MOR

As country music evolved and changed, Nashville pushed back in order to keep and promote the traditional country sounds. This effort was obvious in one of the decade's biggest hits, Glen Campbell's 1975 "Rhinestone Cowboy," recorded with a soaring country-politan string section. With its sentimental lyrics about a battered country singer hoping one day to shine like a rhinestone cowboy, the song rose to number 1 on both the country and pop charts.

Kenny Rogers was one of the most prominent rhinestone-studded country hit makers in the late 1970s. Rogers topped pop and country charts with 1977's "Lucille" and achieved superstar status the following year with "The Gambler." Following this success, Rogers teamed up with Dottie West to record several albums of pop duets that were pure countrypolitan.

As artists such as Campbell and Rogers topped the country and pop charts, the

BLUEGRASS AND THE DEAD

The Grateful Dead, which was formed in 1965 by Jerry Garcia, was a counterculture group inspired by country music. Garcia, the renowned lead guitarist for the Dead, started his career at age 15 by playing the banjo. Like many others of his generation, Garcia listened to the *Grand Ole Opry* on the radio every Saturday night. In the early 1960s, Garcia played bluegrass music in San Francisco coffeehouses and bars.

In 1973, Garcia decided to branch out with Old and In The Way, a band he formed with a group of bluegrass musicians. Old and In The Way played classic bluegrass tunes, such as Monroe's "Uncle Pen," along with original music. Because of his commitment to the Grateful Dead, Garcia could not maintain his leading role in the band. By the time the album *Old and In The Way* was released in 1975, the group had disbanded. Despite its short life, *Old and In The Way* introduced bluegrass to a counterculture audience raised on the Beatles, the Dead, and the Rolling Stones.

The Grateful Dead is one of the most popular bands in music history. Their fans are often referred to as "Deadheads."

ACROSS GENERATIONS AND BARRIERS

In 1972, the California-based Nitty Gritty Dirt Band brought together an all-star lineup of old-time bluegrass musicians for the triple album *Will the Circle Be Unbroken*. The album included established and respected *Grand Ole Opry* stars such as "Mother" Maybelle Carter, Merle Travis, Earl Scruggs, and Jimmy Martin. Other players, such as Doc Watson, Norman Blake, and Vassar Clements, were virtually unknown outside bluegrass circles. Most participants in the project had been forgotten in the early 1970s, when countrypolitan was the main sound issued by Nashville.

Will the Circle Be Unbroken is filled with hot picking, singing, and vocal harmony. Every track was recorded live, and many of the songs are either first or second takes. Without a single sour note or missed lick, the album's raw, rolling bluegrass sound was a hit among a new generation unfamiliar with the *Grand Ole Opry* or its classic stars. The breakout success of the album introduced an entire generation of young rock fans to country music. The increased exposure of bluegrass in the wake of *Will the Circle Be Unbroken* helped the genre continue to grow.

outlaw movement faded away. By 1980, an entirely new philosophy was driving songwriters and performers. No longer were songs rough, edgy, or experimental. Instead, they were written to appeal to as many people at once as possible. Known as middle of the road, or MOR, this new genre of country music was a huge success. It would take some years before country would once again connect with this part of its roots.

Urban Cowboys
and Western Women

By the early 1980s, most country and western hits sounded nothing like the songs that had come before them. MOR songs flourished, filling the radio stations with hour after hour of sweet and sentimental lyrics and lush background notes. Artists such as Debby Boone, Tanya Tucker, Ronnie Milsap, Lee Greenwood, and Janie Fricke had huge hits. Boone's "You Light Up My Life" played every hour, commonly followed closely by Johnny Lee's "Lookin' for Love." Even though countrypolitan stars were selling millions of records, it was easy to understand why music critic Boris Weintraub of the *Washington Star* wrote, "Perhaps it's time to find a new term to replace 'country.' Because, good or bad, there is precious little country left in today's country music."[31]

Over at Gilley's

Boris Weintraub's observation about country music came in the middle of what was called the urban cowboy era. The term was derived from a 1978 article in *Esquire* that described oil workers who spent their nights at a huge honky-tonk in Pasadena, Texas, called Gilley's, owned by outlaw singer Mickey Gilley. The men at Gilley's dressed like cowboys, drank numerous beers, and took turns riding a mechanical bull. The article inspired the 1980 movie *Urban Cowboy*, starring John Travolta and Debra Winger. *Urban Cowboy* was one of the top-grossing films of the era, and the soundtrack, with songs by Gilley, Johnny Lee, the Eagles, Kenny Rogers, and other country acts, went multiplatinum, which means it sold more than 2 million copies.

Urban Cowboy kicked off a fad featuring cowboy boots, Stetson hats, designer blue jeans, and pickup trucks. In response, thousands of bars across the country installed mechanical bulls and hosted nights dedicated to a

By the end of the 20th century, country music had been on the silver screen for decades. The 1980s brought Willie Nelson's *Honeysuckle Rose*, Dolly Parton's *9 to 5*, Loretta Lynn's *Coal Miner's Daughter*, and Patsy Cline's story in *Sweet Dreams*. In the 2000s and 2010s, stories of country music stars are still appearing in such movies as *Walk the Line* (2005), *Crazy Heart* (2009), *Country Strong* (2011), *The Last Ride* (2011), and *I Saw the Light* (2016). Each one of these movies gave insight into country music's history, and many showed mainstream America the life stories of some of the genre's biggest stars. Often, after the release of these movies, country music sales jump as people want to find out more.

two-step country line dance called the Cotton-Eyed Joe. Like all trends, the urban cowboy fad peaked quickly and crashed just as fast. As the urban cowboy and MOR fads faded away, people wondered what country music would do next. Hope was found with a group of talented musicians who grew up around the cotton fields of Fort Payne, Alabama. Guitarist Randy Owen, bassist Teddy Gentry, and keyboard and fiddle player Jeff Cook were cousins. They formed the group Alabama with drummer Mark Herndon in 1977. Raised on traditional honky-tonk, hard country, and country rock, Alabama was determined to put the traditional country sounds of bluegrass and honky-tonk back into country music.

Alabama had its first hit with "Tennessee River" the year *Urban Cowboy* was released. The song has a driving two-step beat; tight three-part harmonies; a distorted rock guitar; and an anthem-like, sing-along chorus. The song also breaks into a lightning-fast fiddle breakdown in the middle, and this musical formula was put to work on Alabama's subsequent releases. This sound appealed to both traditional country music fans and younger fans raised on rock. As Kurt Wolff wrote, "Gently blending pop and country into easily digestible formulas, their sound appeals across generations; they're just rebellious enough for the young folks, but their parents also dig the boys' pretty harmonies, sentimental soft spots, and old-fashioned family values."[32]

Everything Alabama recorded turned to gold. The group had more than 20 hits between 1980 and 1987. In 1989, Alabama won the Artist of the Decade award at the Academy of Country Music (ACM) Awards. By the time Herndon quit in 2007, the band had scored 30 chart-topping hits and sold more than 73 million records.

John Travolta's film Urban Cowboy *brought new life to country music, and the soundtrack was incredibly popular.*

Those sales figures place Alabama among the top-selling acts in music history, a list that includes Elvis Presley, the Beatles, and the Rolling Stones.

Alabama was one of the first bands to gain acceptance in a business that generally promoted individual singers. The group's popularity showed producers that youth-oriented country bands could sell records, and a host of groups such as Sawyer Brown, Southern Pacific, the Desert Rose Band, and the Kentucky Headhunters were promoted throughout the 1980s.

Mother and Daughter

When RCA Records signed the Judds—a mother and daughter group from Kentucky—Naomi Judd was 36, and Wynonna was 18. Two years later, the Judds released "Mama,

Naomi Judd (left) formed a band with her daughter Wynonna (right), while her other daughter, Ashley, went on to become an actress and political activist.

COUNTRY MUSIC: A UNIQUELY AMERICAN SOUND

He's Crazy," a breakout hit single that peaked at number 1 and won the Judds a Grammy for Best Country Vocal by a Duo or Group. With its simple production, acoustic guitar, and dominant pedal steel, the song has an old-time honky-tonk feel. During the next five years, the Judds were unstoppable, recording thirteen more chart-toppers in a row. The music was a blend of traditional country, blues, rock, bluegrass, and pop and helped make the Judds one of the most successful duos in country music history.

Due to ill health, Naomi retired in 1991. Wynonna launched a solo career the following year. Her first album, *Wynonna*, was an immediate smash hit, selling more than 3 million copies. Her next album, *Tell Me Why*, achieved similar success. In 1993, Naomi published her best-selling autobiography, *Love Can Build a Bridge*, which was later turned into a television movie.

Since 2001, Wynonna and Naomi have held periodic musical reunions, which produce sold-out concerts and top-selling songs. In 2009, Wynonna continued her musical journey with *Sing Chapter 1*, an album of vintage pop, country, and swing songs that showcase the bluesy voice that drove the Judds' sound for a quarter century. In 2016, she released *Wynonna & the Big Noise*, which features everything from blues to country pop. It was her first time recording without many rehearsals, and it was difficult for her. "I just got in the studio in front of that microphone and sang from my toenails," she told *Rolling Stone*. "I let whatever came to me just fly."[33]

The mother and daughter toured once more in 2010 and filmed the documentary series *The Judds*. The music of the Judds was part of the latest country music style known as neotraditional, new traditional, or new country. The genre was a reaction to the overproduced country music from the *Urban Cowboy* era. Interestingly, the biggest stars of new country were not based in Nashville but in Texas, Oklahoma, and even California. These neotraditionalists fueled the biggest commercial boom in country music history.

A Founding Father

George Strait is one of the founding fathers of the neotraditional movement. Born in 1952, Strait grew up on a huge Texas cattle ranch. He formed a country band, Ace in the Hole, in 1975. Strait's music was strongly influenced by the western swing of Bob Wills, the hard-core honky-tonk tradition of Hank Williams, the barroom ballads of Lefty Frizzell, and the Bakersfield sound of Merle Haggard.

Strait released his first single, "Unwound," in 1981 and followed with the album *Strait Country*. Both quickly reached number 1. According to music journalist David Dicaire, "Strait's record drew deeply from the honky tonk tradition, bypassing the trappings of lush country-pop crossovers, Outlaw, *Urban Cowboy* swagger and country-rock; it pointed the genre to a new future direction."[34]

Throughout the 1980s, every one of Strait's albums contained at least one number-1 single and reached either gold or platinum status. By 2011, he had sold nearly 69 million albums and accumulated 58 number-1 singles, breaking a record for solo country music artists previously held by Conway Twitty. Strait was also nominated for more Country Music Association and Academy of Country Music awards than any other artist. Strait was among the first country superstars to emerge from the late 20th century, leading the charge for the breakout hits of 1989.

The Class of '89

Performers Alan Jackson, Garth Brooks, Clint Black, Dwight Yoakam, and Travis Tritt were all considered members of the Class of '89—all of their first hits occurred that year. These singers had roots in neotraditionalism but infused their music with a youthful sound and a rock-and-roll feel. The Class of '89 valued musical virtuosity and honesty. The neotraditionalists looked to the elders of country music for their inspiration. Their sounds relied on rich, Southern-accented vocals sung over driving rock drumbeats, hot-picking electric guitars, and screaming fiddles. The orchestrated string sections and syrupy backup vocals that dominated country just a few years earlier were nowhere to be found.

While the Class of '89 based their sound on musical honesty, their image was pure entertainment. With the growing popularity of CMT in the early 1990s, the music videos produced by the new country artists featured what Kurt Wolff described as "hunks in hats, pretty gals in boots, and bright-eyed freshly scrubbed faces."[35]

While some in Nashville were not pleased with new country's flash, few could argue with its astonishing financial success. Driven by the growing popularity of music videos, country album sales doubled from $500 million annually to $1 billion between 1989 and 1991. They doubled again by 1995, and by 1996, two out of every three albums on the country charts achieved gold, platinum, or multiplatinum status.

A Record Executive's Dream

Oklahoma-born Garth Brooks was at the head of country music's economic boom in the 1990s. His 1991 album *Ropin' the Wind* debuted at number 1 on the pop and country charts—the first country album to ever do so—and eventually sold more than 10 million copies. Brooks was a record executive's dream. With his down-home personality, he put his family first and, similarly to George Strait, represented the humble and endearing values of country music.

When he strapped on his guitar and took to the stage, however, Brooks took his cues more from rocker Bruce Springsteen than from Hank Williams. He jumped, danced, strutted, swung from the rafters on cables, and occasionally smashed his guitar—all the while singing into his headset microphone. This brand of hard-rocking country appealed to a huge audience of country fans.

By drawing crowds more associated with rock music festivals and by selling more than 66 million albums throughout the 1990s, Brooks changed the country music industry. For example, Brooks attracted more than 200,000 people to New York City's Central Park for a free concert in 1997, and by the end of

FROM CIRCLES TO LINES

People have been dancing to the fiddles, guitars, and mandolins of country music for centuries. Historically—in many rural regions of the United States—the Saturday-night square dance at a local barn was one of the few sources of entertainment. Line dancing, which originated centuries ago, was also popular. Line dancing involves a large group of people arranged in a line facing the same direction, executing coordinated dance steps.

In 1992, the popularity of line dancing reached dizzying heights thanks to country singer Billy Ray Cyrus. His song "Achy Breaky Heart," with its driving two-step beat, peaked on both country and pop charts. The video, shown in heavy rotation on CMT, stars a large group of people line dancing at one of Cyrus's concerts, and it helped make the dance style a national craze. Around the same time, the country music duo Brooks & Dunn released "Boot Scootin' Boogie," a tribute to the Texas honky-tonk line dancing style. In the years that followed, country dance halls filled with line dancers dressed in tight jeans, cowboy boots, and western shirts and hats. By the end of the 1990s, thousands of country line dancing clubs were spread across the United States, and dancers could learn steps from countless online videos and dance classes.

the 1990s, he was selling out stadiums in a matter of minutes. In the years since, Brooks has only grown in country music. He has won half a dozen CMA Entertainer of the Year awards, and in 2018, he was inducted into the Live Music Hall of Fame. "It's a total shock and quite an honor," he said at the ceremony. "I don't think an entertainer is anything without the people who allow him to do this."[36] He and his country and western singing wife, Trisha Yearwood, continue to thrill fans of all ages across the globe. Brooks's success helped to create a demand for other country acts such as Clint Black, Alan Jackson, and Vince Gill, who all had their roots in neotraditionalism but whose beat was closer to country rock.

Influential Women in Country Music

When Canadian Shania Twain arrived on the scene in 1993, she quickly became the most controversial of the new country artists. Born in Ontario, Canada, Twain starred in music videos featuring outfits that often seemed to be mimicking the pop star Madonna.

Twain's music endeared her to country music fans raised on rock and roll and music videos. Her producer and then-husband, Robert John "Mutt" Lange, previously worked with hard rock bands such as Def Leppard and AC/DC. Lange's rock-and-roll roots can be heard in Twain's unique sound, blending new country, pop, honky-tonk, rockabilly, and swing.

Twain's second album, *The Woman in Me,* has sold more than 20 million copies, and her third album, *Come on Over,* has sold more than 40 million copies—making her the first female artist to reach such immense numbers. By 2018, Twain had sold more than 100 million records. Although she officially retired in 2004 due to illness, she turned her health struggle into a television miniseries and autobiography. In 2015, she returned to touring and in 2017, she released the album *Now.* Over the years, Twain has won multiple Grammys and has been inducted into the Canadian Music Hall of Fame.

Neotraditional country and western singers included many important women such as Shania Twain, the Judds, k. d. lang, and Nanci Griffith. Griffith, a singer-songwriter from Texas, infused her country music with the understated acoustic sounds of folk to create a sound she dubbed folkabilly. Griffith lived in Nashville for a short time in 1985, where she wrote songs for other artists. One Griffith song, "Love

A POWERFUL VOICE

Of all the neotraditionalist singers, k. d. lang may be the most distinctive. In the late 1980s, lang's amazingly rich, textured voice and authentic 1940s and 1950s country sound attracted widespread attention. Her 1988 album *Shadowland* and 1989 album *Absolute Torch and Twang* were both awarded gold records. The albums held a unique status, topping both the mainstream country charts and the alternative underground charts occupied by alt-rock groups such as R.E.M. and Sonic Youth. Since then, she has produced 11 additional albums, including one in which she performed with legendary singer Tony Bennett. In 2016, she released an album that is a compilation of songs with singers Neko Case and Laura Veirs titled *case/lang/veirs*.

One reason for k. d. lang's success in the country music business is her desire to be unique.

at the Five and Dime," was a hit for country artist Kathy Mattea in 1986, while "Outbound Plane" was a chart topper for Suzy Bogguss in 1991. Despite her success, Griffith was unhappy with the Nashville music establishment and preferred to record her own brand of critically acclaimed folkabilly without the input of Music City veterans.

Two other women who played the new traditional style—Carlene Carter and Rosanne Cash—are stepsisters who both grew up in Nashville. They are referred to as country royalty because of their musical family heritage. Carlene Carter is the daughter of 1950s honky-tonk star Carl Smith and June Carter Cash, who is the daughter of Maybelle Carter, member of the pioneering country music group the Carter Family. Rosanne Cash is the child of Johnny Cash and his first wife, Vivian. (June Carter married Johnny Cash in 1968, after the girls were born.)

Carlene Carter blended country, rock, swing, rockabilly, and honky-tonk on her 1990 breakthrough album *I Fell in Love*. Her sound was achieved with a cast of country and rock luminaries that included guitarist James Burton, who backed Elvis Presley; drummer Jim Keltner, who played with John Lennon after the Beatles broke up; and backup singer Nicolette Larson, who sang with Neil Young as well as recorded her own best-selling album.

Rosanne Cash also experimented with various styles, playing traditional country on the album *Seven Year Ache*, then shocked Nashville—and many of her fans—by recording the new wave–tinged *Rhythm and Romance*. As the daughter of Johnny Cash, she was able to follow her own musical instincts in a city bound by tradition. In doing so, Rosanne Cash topped the country charts 11 times in the 1980s.

A Girl from Oklahoma

Reba McEntire was another artist who rejected the Nashville sound to achieve success. Born in Oklahoma, McEntire grew up riding at rodeo events. She moved to Nashville in 1974, but she achieved only minor success for a decade. McEntire finally became a major star when she embraced neotraditionalism in 1984. The record *My Kind of Country* was McEntire's eighth album but the first one on which she asserts her own identity, ironically, while covering old honky-tonk favorites by Ray Price, Faron Young, and Connie Smith. McEntire's traditional arrangements and expressive voice, which convey sorrow, anger, and joy, helped her unite with the neotraditionalists.

In 1984, McEntire won the prestigious Female Vocalist of the Year award from the CMAs, beating superstars such as Dolly Parton and Barbara Mandrell. By the end of the 1980s, McEntire's brand of neotraditionalism made her one of the top-selling acts of the era, and her success rolled on for decades. Today, she is not only a country music icon with gold, platinum, and multiplatinum records, she is also an actress. In addition to

Reba McEntire has won many awards for her music.

appearing in a number of films, she was the star of her own TV show, *Reba*, from 2001 to 2007, as well as several other television series. She won the Female Vocalist of the Year award at the CMAs four times between 1984 and 1987. Her popularity is still strong into the 21st century, and she played Colonel Sanders in several Kentucky Fried Chicken commercials, beginning in 2018.

Success and Shame

Sisters Martie and Emily Erwin were musicians—Martie was a fiddle player, while Emily played banjo, guitar, Dobro, accordion, and bass. When they added in Laura Lynch on upright bass and guitarist Robin Lynn Macy, the women formed the Dixie Chicks.

The Dixie Chicks built a following playing at bluegrass festivals and opening for major acts such as Garth Brooks, Reba McEntire, and George Strait. In 1992, Natalie Maines joined the group as lead singer after Lynch and Macy dropped out. As a trio, the Dixie Chicks utilized the old-time bluegrass sound of fiddle, banjo, and guitar. The group maintained only moderate success until 1998, when their album *Wide Open Spaces* quickly sold 6 million copies, shooting it to the top of the Billboard country charts. Sales were boosted by the band's clever videos, in heavy rotation on CMT, which featured the attractive young artists showing off their musical skills while clowning around in airports, on tour buses, and onstage.

The Dixie Chicks' sound has been described as neo—or new—bluegrass, popular with both country and pop audiences. In a business geared toward a conservative, middle-aged population, the Dixie Chicks were notable because more than half of their records sold to people younger than 30. Maines damaged the band's reputation among traditional country fans, however, when on March 10, 2003—just nine days before the United States invaded Iraq—she criticized President George W. Bush, a fellow Texan. From the stage at a small club in London, England, she exclaimed, "Just so you know, we're on the good side with y'all. We do not want this war, this violence, and we're ashamed that the President of the United States is from Texas."[37]

An uproar followed once Maines's statement hit the media. The Dixie Chicks received countless death threats, their songs were banned from radio stations, their music was boycotted, and the group was loudly booed at their following concerts. In several cities, Dixie Chicks CDs were burned or crushed by bulldozers at public events sponsored by radio personalities. The entire controversy was covered in the 2006 documentary *Dixie Chicks: Shut Up and Sing*.

Although Maines later apologized for her comments, the Dixie Chicks lost many fans among the conservative crowds in Nashville. The Dixie Chicks returned in 2016 for the 53-city tour *DCX MMXVI*, hoping that their fan base was still around to support them. Concerts quickly sold out, and many country fans are lovingly accepting the group back into their hearts—and onto their favorite radio stations.

CHAPTER SEVEN

Changing
with the Times

Where is it possible to find 750,000 or more bluegrass fans all in one place? If it is October and in San Francisco's Golden Gate Park, the answer is simple: the *Hardly Strictly Bluegrass* festival. Here, performers stand on everything—from huge stages to in front of outfitted airplanes—and play and sing for the crowd. The free event lasts for three days and is the highlight concert of the year for bluegrass fans across the globe. Blankets are tossed, Frisbees are thrown, people dance, food is sold, and the air is full of the sounds of acoustic guitars, mandolins, fiddles, pedal steel guitars, and stand-up basses. For those three days, everyone gives in to summer afternoons of relaxation.

The bluegrass festival began in October 2001 and featured Emmylou Harris and Alison Krauss. The *Strictly Bluegrass* festival—as it was first named—was the brainchild of Warren Hellman, a billionaire venture capitalist, banjo player, and bluegrass enthusiast. The first concert was a huge success. By 2002, the event had grown to two days and the roster of acts included Harris, Peter Rowan, and a wide array of progressive bluegrass acts with names such as Belle Monroe & Her Brewglass Boys.

In 2004, Hellman felt the name "Strictly Bluegrass" limited the scope of the festival. He added the word "Hardly" to the name and added a third day of festivities. In the following years, the *Hardly Strictly Bluegrass* (HSB) festival became a showcase for 21st century country music. The lineup featured respected veterans such as Merle Haggard and Earl Scruggs alongside a wide array of younger country acts such as Southern Culture on the Skids, Neko Case, Béla Fleck, and Gillian Welch.

Each year, the Hardly Strictly Bluegrass *festival brings together thousands of bluegrass music fans and some of the world's best bluegrass bands.*

Alison Krauss

Many of the stars who have appeared at *HSB* are known as progressive bluegrass musicians. Their fresh sounds have contributed to the 21st century bluegrass revival. Rather than rehashing the music of Bill Monroe and Earl Scruggs, progressive bluegrass players added new chord changes, tempos, and attitudes to a beloved style.

One of the leading artists of the bluegrass revival, Alison Krauss, was born in 1971 and grew up in Decatur, Illinois. She began entering fiddle contests at a young age, and at 14 years old, Krauss was signed to a recording contract. In addition to her genius fiddle playing, Krauss has a high

A DARK ATMOSPHERE

With her searing vocals and quirky songs, Neko Case's music and songwriting blends the best of Loretta Lynn, Hank Williams, and even Bob Dylan. Through her music, she delivers toe-tapping mediations, dark alt-country despair, and blue midnight moods. Case was born in Alexandria, Virginia, in 1970, and launched a cross-border career in 1994 that spanned Tacoma, Washington; Seattle; and Vancouver, Canada. Her highly acclaimed 1997 debut album, *The Virginian*, has a smoky, reverb-drenched 1950s feel, with Case covering songs by Lynn and Ernest Tubb.

Case's next two albums, *Furnace Room Lullaby* (2000) and *Blacklisted* (2002), contain material she wrote or co-wrote. On these records, Case's echoing, minor-key songs are cinematic, invoking images from old cowboy movies. The albums earned widespread accolades from critics and fans alike.

Case became a favorite on late-night talk shows, such as *Late Night with Jimmy Fallon*, and the publicity helped her 2009 album—*Middle Cyclone*—reach number 3 on the Billboard charts. It was her first album to crack the top 10. Since then, she has produced three other albums: *The Worse Things Get, the Harder I Fight, the Harder I Fight, the More I Love You* came out in 2013; that was followed three years later with a collaboration album with singers k. d. lang, and Laura Veirs. In 2018, Case released *Hell-On* and went on a tour to promote it. Critics agree that Case could have easily been a huge country pop star if she so chose. However, she remained true to her unique vision and produced honest music with a darker perspective than many other country musicians embrace.

soprano voice that Dicaire described as "truly angelic … her vocal range is suited to the material she often sings, which is about lost love."[38]

Throughout the early 1990s, Krauss alternated between recording with her band—Union Station—and making solo albums. In 1995, she attained a level of success no traditional bluegrass act had ever accomplished. Her album *Now That I've Found You: A Collection* went double platinum, and she won four CMA awards, including Best Single, Best Female Vocalist, and New Artist of the Year. Krauss also won two Grammys.

Krauss's success continued well into the 21st century. In 2000, she expanded her fan base with her three-song contribution to the multiplatinum soundtrack for the movie *O Brother, Where Art Thou?* In 2004, her album with Union Station, *Lonely Runs Both Ways*, achieved double platinum status driven by two number-1 hits: "Restless" and

Alison Krauss often plays to enormous crowds at large outdoor festivals.

"If I Didn't Know Any Better." In 2007, Krauss strengthened her alt-country credentials recording the album *Raising Sand* with Robert Plant, best known as the wailing lead singer of the 1970s hard-rock supergroup Led Zeppelin. *Raising Sand* received extensive critical acclaim and won five Grammy awards, including Album of the Year. By this time, Krauss had won more Grammy awards than any other female artist in history. In 2011, she released *Paper Airplane*, which was awarded with two more Grammys, and in 2017, she released her first solo album since 1999: *Windy City*. Krauss's many awards have been earned because she gave old sounds a fresh new take. This promoted the bluegrass revival and popularized the sound of fiddles, mandolins, and Dobros in a new century.

Lucinda Williams

Alternative country, or alt-country, is another popular new sound at *HSB*. Alt-country describes artists who combine a wide variety of sounds, including honky-tonk, rock, blues, punk, and other musical elements. The sound is lively, edgy, and rarely heard on country radio. Alt-country singers often have a less-polished vocal sound, and their raw musical arrangements give the feeling of a live performance.

An example of the alt-country sound is the 1998 Grammy-winning album *Car Wheels on a Gravel Road* by Lucinda Williams, a true star in the alt-country genre. Williams delayed the release of the album for several years because she had a problem with the overproduced Nashville sound of her vocals. After a long battle with her record company, Williams moved production to California, where she was able to achieve the sound she desired. AllMusic reviewer Steve Huey explained, "The production ... throws Williams' idiosyncratic voice into sharp relief, to the point where it's noticeably separate from the band. As a result, every inflection and slight tonal alteration is captured."[39]

Beyond nurturing unique production values, Williams also writes mesmerizing lyrics that explore uncomfortable topics rarely covered in modern country music. The song "Drunken Angel," for example, is about a talented but broken-down musician who is shot and killed in a senseless argument. "Concrete and Barbed Wire" is written from the viewpoint of a woman whose boyfriend is in prison. "Greenville" details a woman's heartbreaking relationship with an abusive, drunken musician.

There is no denying Lucinda Williams has created a unique sound that could not be confused with any other artist. After the success of *Car Wheels on a Gravel Road*, Williams pursued an even more stripped-down sound. Her 2001 follow-up album, *Essence*, is filled with laid-back songs that, for the most part, highlight Williams's voice and acoustic guitar. The bluesy songs on 2003's *World Without Tears* feature teary lyrics, slow-tempo songs, and spare arrangements. Between 2005 and 2017, Williams released several albums, including *Little Honey*, which featured guest artists such as Elvis Costello and Susanna Hoffs, and the double album *Down Where the Spirit Meets the Bone*.

The Patriotism of Toby Keith

Toby Keith started his career in

1993 as a contemporary of new country artists Garth Brooks and Alan Jackson. As a young man growing up in Clinton, Oklahoma, in the 1970s, he was inspired by Bob Wills and Merle Haggard. Keith produced several platinum albums in the late 1990s, but his fame exploded when he expressed his political beliefs in 2002. Keith wrote the song "Courtesy of the Red, White and Blue (The Angry American)" as a response to the terrorist attacks of September 11, 2001. The song is about waving the flag, the Statue of Liberty shaking her fist in anger, and seeking justice. This stirred up widespread discussion and made Keith a household name. Hardcore country fans propelled the single to number 1, and it also crossed over to the pop charts.

Keith followed his successful single in 2003 with *Shock'n Y'all*. The album contains the songs "American Soldier" and "The Taliban Song." The politics are tempered by upbeat honky-tonk anthems spread throughout the album. Although Keith gained attention for his angry songs, politics are not his main concern, as Stephen Thomas Erlewine explained:

> Since Toby Keith not only can come across as a loudmouth redneck but seems to enjoy being a loudmouth redneck, it's easy for some listeners to dismiss him

... *Those listeners aren't entirely wrong, since he can succumb to reactionary politics ... He's an old-fashioned, cantankerous outlaw who's eager to be as oversized and larger than life as legends like Waylon Jennings, Merle Haggard, and Willie Nelson, who bucked conventions and spoke their minds.*[40]

Whatever Keith's motivations, his songs continued to top the country music charts every year throughout the 2000s and into the 2010s. Keith's 15th studio album, 2011's *Clancy's Tavern*, featured the number-1 single "Made In America," a song about an old farming couple who will only buy products made in the United States. A second song from the album, "Red Solo Cup," balances out the political statements with an upbeat party song. The "Red Solo Cup" video went viral on YouTube, and it has more than 40 million views. Keith produced three more albums over the next few years, including *35 MPH Town* in 2015.

Keith makes a point of backing his political words with patriotic actions. Between 2005 and 2011, the country singer participated in nine weeklong USO tours where he entertained American troops in Iraq, in Afghanistan, and at sea on aircraft carriers. Unlike some USO entertainers who only play on large bases, Keith insisted on playing at forward-operating bases in the middle of dangerous war zones. Commenting on his dedication to American soldiers, Keith stated, "Since my first tour, I've been hooked on performing for troops. I start looking forward to my next USO trip the minute I touch down here in the States. I love it and I love our troops, they are the best in the world."[41]

Chesney's Country Roots

Kenny Chesney had 15 albums under his belt by 2008, and he was producing top-10 hits every year. While Keith's style stuck close to his neotraditional honky-tonk roots, Chesney's music changed over time. While he started out in 1993 with a neotraditional and hard-country style, Chesney spent the following years sailing his yacht in the Caribbean and living in the Virgin Islands, where he heard reggae and calypso music. It inspired him to infuse his style with Caribbean sounds, making it unique on country radio.

Chesney's first move in a new direction can be heard on the 2002 pop-crossover hit single "On the Coast of Somewhere Beautiful," from the album *No Shoes, No Shirt, No Problems*. The record, with its drifting sailboat feel, established a new sound for Chesney. His follow-up album, *When the Sun Goes Down*, was saturated with laid-back island music in a style perfected by pop star Jimmy Buffett in the 1980s.

Chesney remained true to his country roots as he continued to blend radio-friendly country with songs about being on the beach, palm trees, and tropical islands. The 2005 album *Be As You Are* is a good example of this mix, with slow, sentimental country pop songs such as "Old Blue Chair" next to island calypso rockers such as "Guitars and Tiki Bars." In 2008, Chesney combined country, rock, and reggae beats in "Everybody Wants to Go to Heaven." Between 2008 and 2018, Chesney released five more albums—from *Welcome to the Fishbowl*, which features a song with Grace Potter, to 2016's *Cosmic Hallelujah*.

Fearless Taylor Swift

While older, experienced musicians—including Chesney, Brad Paisley, and Krauss—played for mature fans in the 2000s, one of their biggest competitors, Taylor Swift, was a young woman barely out of high school. Swift's talent for writing songs about boys and growing up appealed to teenage girls. This coveted audience bought a lot of Swift's albums, attended many concerts,

Kenny Chesney's fans are eager to be close to their music idol,
as demonstrated at this concert in Detroit, Michigan.

and purchased mountains of T-shirts and other merchandise.

Swift was born in 1989—the same year Garth Brooks and Alan Jackson released their first albums. A native of Pennsylvania, Swift was only 11 when she traveled to Nashville with dreams of obtaining a major record deal. Although she visited every company on Music Row with a demo tape, Swift returned home unsuccessful. To help her pursue her career, Swift's family moved to Nashville. Her luck soon improved: In 2003, 14-year-old Swift's songwriting talents impressed executives at Sony/ATV. She was hired as a staff songwriter, making her the youngest person to ever hold that job.

When not working, Swift performed at the Bluebird Café, a Nashville songwriter's showcase. A talent scout for the newly formed label Big Machine Records spotted her, and she was signed to a recording contract in 2005. The following year, at the age of 16, Swift released her first single, "Tim McGraw," a wistful song about a lost love. The music video, which shows Swift in a field with a handsome boy, catapulted the talented young country singer to instant stardom and became a staple on CMT.

Swift's debut smash single was soon followed by the album *Taylor Swift*. It quickly peaked at number 1 on the Billboard Top Country Album charts and crossed over to peak at number 5 on the Billboard 200 pop charts. In what was an unusual move for a country act, the album's second chart-topping single, "Teardrops On My Guitar," was released in two separate versions. One was a smooth mix for country radio. The second featured a stronger beat and vocal arrangement meant for pop audiences. Three more singles from *Taylor Swift* sold more than 1 million copies each. In 2007, she was so popular that she was booked to open concerts for several top country artists, including Rascal Flatts, Brad Paisley, and George Strait.

When Swift released her second album, *Fearless*, in November 2008, it had the largest opening for any female artist in any musical category that year. Five singles from *Fearless* entered the top 10 on both the country and pop charts. Swift's winning streak continued in 2009 as she won numerous awards, including Best Female Video from MTV and Album of the Year from the ACM. Swift was also the youngest artist—and one of only seven women—to ever win the CMA's highest honor: the award for Entertainer of the Year.

Swift's astounding accomplishments continued when her third studio album, *Speak Now*, sold more than 1 million copies the week after its October 2010 release. By August 2011, sales totaled more than 5.5 million. Like previous Swift efforts, the album blends acoustic country, soft rock, and catchy pop production values. In 2012, Swift released *Red* with the huge hit "We Are Never Ever Getting Back Together." It was followed two years later by *1989* and one of Swift's biggest singles, "Shake It Off." In 2017, *Reputation* was released with the lead single "Look What You Made Me Do."

Since the release of *Red*, Swift's musical style has become more and more pop-oriented. Her mature songwriting skills and lyrics have an undeniable appeal to a large segment of the country audience, but rather than writing crossover hits, many believe Swift has truly "crossed over" and become a pop performer—not a country musician.

Nonetheless, the dedication of Swift's fans was obvious in 2015 when her *1989* tour pulled in more than $250 million, breaking the North American record of $162 million, set by the Rolling Stones in 2005. During that tour, she appeared in 53 cities, did 83 performances, and sold nearly 2.3 million tickets.

Carrie Underwood

Another powerful, country-singing woman is Carrie Underwood. Born in Muskogee, Oklahoma, in 1983, Underwood learned to play guitar and piano at a young age, developed a three-octave singing range, and performed at local events throughout her childhood. In 2005, she was a contestant on *American Idol*. Underwood's charm and strong, pure vocal style helped make her the first country singer to win the competition. Her debut single, "Inside Your Heaven," was released soon after.

Thanks to her national television exposure, Underwood's first album, *Some Hearts*, sold more than 300,000 copies in its first week. The album went on to sell more than 8 million total copies, making it one of 2006's best-selling records. Unlike Swift, Underwood did not write any of the 14 songs on her first album. For the follow-up, *Carnival Ride*, Underwood decided to become more involved in the songwriting process. She collaborated with a group of professional Nashville songwriters and co-wrote three songs on the 2007 effort. The album debuted at number 1 on the pop charts and soon went triple platinum. Underwood's third album—2009's *Play On*—achieved similar success. Her following albums, *Blown Away* (2012), *Storyteller* (2015), and *Cry Pretty* (2018) have produced hit singles such as "Two Black Cadillacs," "Heartbeat," and "Church Bells." By 2010, Underwood had gathered even more country music industry awards than Swift, with 10 ACM awards compared to Swift's 3 ACM awards.

Old Favorites and Breakout Hits

While some stars attract far more attention from their fans, there are hundreds of artists, new and old, who keep bringing joy to country music fans. As fast as one performer rises on the charts, another is waiting right behind. Recent years have seen some incredible country groups—from Lady Antebellum to Little Big Town. Individual singers, including Brad Paisley, Keith Urban, and Jason Aldean, have hit singles and fill country and western radio stations with their new sounds and innovative styles.

Carrie Underwood's performances continue to win her more fans—and more awards.

COUNTRY MUSIC: A UNIQUELY AMERICAN SOUND

In 2017, *Rolling Stone* magazine announced 10 new country artists that fans should keep an eye—and ear—on. On the top of the list was OSMR, or Old Southern Moonshine Revival. A three-man group, OSMR focuses on fast finger-picking on guitars and playful lyrics. Marcus Kiser, the group's lead singer, has said, "We're more or less a rock band with a country lyric, and a country vocal."[42] The group first rose to prominence around 2015, when their song "Waste Another Beer" received a lot of airtime on satellite radio stations across the United States. Their fast paced and exciting blend of rock and country has acquired a huge following, and their popularity is set to continue expanding well beyond the 2010s.

Another up-and-coming country star is Ashley McBryde. The world of country music—especially for female singers—has traditionally focused on performers who break onto the scene in their 20s. McBryde, however, spent her 20s building up an underground following, and her first major record—*Girl Going Nowhere*—was released in 2018, when she was 34. Because she spent so much time on the stages of small bars and semiprofessional venues, her voice and style have had time to grow and mature. Her powerful singing is accompanied by subtle, but catchy, guitar and bass rhythms.

Taking a more traditionalist country approach, Texas performer Dalton Domino made a name for himself after he quit drinking and drugs all at once—and then wrote a record titled *Corners*. Locked up in a friend's house, he said, "I just sat in a room and wrote these songs."[43] Similarly to legendary performer Johnny Cash, critics and audiences alike have responded positively to the singer-songwriter after he addressed his substance abuse. Before his sobriety and the release of *Corners*, Domino made a name for himself by performing in Lubbock, Texas, picking up some classic Texas styles and blending them with his hometown Memphis, Tennessee, roots.

In addition to solo singer-songwriters, there are some exciting country-rock bands well worth watching. Among the biggest is the Drugstore Gypsies, honky-tonkers who are a perfect accompaniment for a country music fan's gathering with friends. "The biggest root of our sound is rock & roll,"[44] explained front man Duke Ryan. With a strong foundation of driving electric guitars and a steady bass beat, the group adds on layers of country twang and traditional lyrical themes. The Drugstore Gypsies, like many soon-to-be stars, have built a strong following by playing small venues across the South before releasing their debut album. Their self-titled first album—released in 2017—also heavily features trumpets and keyboards, uncommon instruments in the genre as a whole.

Talented fiddler and singer Phoebe Hunt is taking the classic country-style instrument and blending it with folk, gypsy jazz, Texas swing, and more to create her own unique style. "This is what American music truly is," Hunt argued. "It's a melting pot of all these different cultures, inspired by all the places I've been and all the different types of music I've studied."[45] Her 2017 album *Shanti's Shadow* was inspired by her travels in India, and the musical combinations Hunt showcases are both unique and familiar. The sound of the fiddle has long been tied strongly to the country genre, but her new approach to incorporating numerous styles makes her music one of a kind.

Country music has changed tremendously over the decades. Lyrics, notes, and musical styles have shifted and evolved to reflect the times. The original styles first played in the Appalachian Mountains have been transformed. From lush three-part harmonies to countrypolitan, from the comfortable neutrality of middle-of-the-road to edgy, controversial messages, country music is there. Turn on the radio and listen. The songs, regardless of style, will come from the heart, tell a great story, and perhaps even inspire a few to let go and dance.

Notes

Introduction:
Country Music Then and Now

1. *The Washington Post*, "Country Music Television Evolves while Sticking to Its Core Audience," *Denver Post*, April 14, 2016. www.denverpost.com/2016/03/02/country-music-television-evolves-while-sticking-to-its-core-audience/.

Chapter One:
Early Country Music

2. The Carter Family Fold, "The Carter Fold," The Carter Family Fold, accessed on May 14, 2018. www.carterfamilyfold.org/p0001.html.

3. Quoted in Alan Gevinson, "Broadcasting Longevity," Teaching History, accessed on May 14, 2018. teachinghistory.org/history-content/ask-a-historian/14557.

4. Quoted in Jeffrey J. Lange, *Smile When You Call Me a Hillbilly: Country Music's Struggle for Respectability, 1939–1954*. Athens, GA: University of Georgia Press, 2004, p. 59.

5. Quoted in George D. Hay, "A Story of the *Grand Ole Opry*," in *The Bill Monroe Reader*. Ed. Tom Ewing. Chicago, IL: University of Illinois Press, 2000, p. 11.

6. Quoted in Doug Benson, "Bill Monroe: King of Blue Grass Music," in *The Bill Monroe Reader*, p. 33.

7. Quoted in Richard Harrington, "The Blue Bluegrass of Home," *Washington Post*, September 10, 1996. www.washingtonpost.com/archive/lifestyle/1996/09/10/the-blue-bluegrass-of-home/923d4e6c-9bb2-4a41-8911-14e09b263fbf/?utm_term=.3252e830ad51.

8. Quoted in Robert Cantwell, *Bluegrass Breakdown: The Making of the Old Southern Sound*. Chicago, IL: University of Illinois Press, 1984, p. 68.

9.   Bob Artis, *Bluegrass.* New York, NY: Hawthorn Books, 1975, p. 25.

10. David Menconi, "MerleFest Doesn't Want to be Bigger, Just Better," *News & Observer*, April 21, 2017. www.newsobserver. com/entertainment/music-news-reviews/on-the-beat-blog/ article145967449.html.

11. Bluegrass Music Hall of Fame and Museum, "Bluegrass Museum Renamed Bluegrass Music Hall of Fame and Museum," *Cision*, April 17, 2018. www.prnewswire.com/news-releases/ bluegrass-museum-renamed-bluegrass-music-hall-of-fame-- museum-300631538.html.

Chapter Two:
Cowboys and Western Swing

12. Quoted in Dierdre Lannon, "Allen, Jules Verne," in *Handbook of Texas Music.* Ed. Laurie E. Jasinski. Denton, TX: Texas State Historical Association, 2012, PDF e-book.

13. Bill C. Malone and Tracey E. W. Laird, *Country Music USA.* Austin, TX: University of Texas Press, 2002, p. 170.

14. Katy June-Friesen, "The Cowboy in Country Music," *Smithsonian*, September 7, 2011. www.smithsonianmag.com/arts-culture/the- cowboy-in-country-music-71339427.

15. Kurt Wolff, *Country Music: The Rough Guide.* London, UK: Rough Guides, 2000, p. 76.

16. Wolff, *Country Music,* p. 94.

17. Quoted in Charles R. Townsend, *San Antonio Rose: The Life and Music of Bob Wills.* Chicago, IL: University of Illinois Press, 1976, p. 269.

18. Richard Carter, "It Don't Mean a Thing if It Ain't Got That Western Swing," *Times Record News*, June 12, 2017. www.timesrecordnews. com/story/entertainment/music/2017/06/12/dont-mean-thing-if- aint-got-western-swing/102777556.

Chapter Three:
Sin and Sorrow

19. Quoted in Lange, *Smile,* p. 163.

20. Quoted in Nick Tosches, *Country: The Twisted Roots of Rock 'n' Roll.* New York, NY: Da Capo Press, 1985, PDF e-book.

21. Quoted in Country Music Foundation, *Country: The Music and Musicians*. New York, NY: Country Music Foundation Press, 1988, p. 233.
22. Wolff, *Country Music*, pp. 158–159.
23. Quoted in Nicholas Dawidoff, *In the Country of Country: A Journey to the Roots of American Music*. New York, NY: Pantheon Books, 1997, p. 64.

Chapter Four:
The National Music Throne of Nashville

24. Quoted in Diane Pecknold, *The Selling Sound: The Rise of the Country Music Industry*. Durham, NC: Duke University Press, 2007, p. 90.
25. Quoted in Vivien Green Fryd, "'The Sad Twang of Mountain Voices': Thomas Hart Benton's *Sources of Country Music*," in *Reading Country Music: Steel Guitars, Opry Stars, and Honky-tonk Bars*. Ed. Cecelia Tichi. Durham, NC: Duke University Press, 1998, p. 274.
26. Wolff, *Country Music*, p. 315.

Chapter Five:
Music City and the Counterculture

27. Quoted in LeRoy Ashby, *With Amusement for All: A History of American Popular Culture Since 1830*. Lexington, KY: University Press of Kentucky, 2006, p. 384.
28. Bob Dylan, *Chronicles*, vol. 1. New York, NY: Simon & Schuster, 2004, PDF e-book.
29. Barry Gifford, "The Byrds: *Sweetheart of the Rodeo*," *Rolling Stone*, August 14, 1968. www.rollingstone.com/music/albumreviews/sweetheart-of-the-rodeo-19680814.
30. Keith Richards, *Life*. New York, NY: Little, Brown and Company, 2010, PDF e-book.

Chapter Six:
Urban Cowboys and Western Women

31. Quoted in Wolff, *Country Music*, p. 424.
32. Wolff, *Country Music*, p. 429.

33. Quoted in Stephen L.Betts, "Wynonna Recruits Jason Isbell for Self-Titled New Album," *Rolling Stone*, November 6, 2015. www.rollingstone.com/music/news/wynonna-recruits-jason-isbell-for-self-titled-new-album-20151106.

34. David Dicaire, *The New Generation of Country Music Stars: Biographies of 50 Artists Born After 1940*. Jefferson, NC: McFarland & Company, 2008, p. 7.

35. Wolff, *Country Music,* p. 502.

36. Quoted in Jeff Gage, "Garth Brooks Named First Inductee into Live Hall of Fame," *Rolling Stone*, February 9, 2018. www.rollingstone.com/country/news/garth-brooks-named-first-inductee-into-live-hall-of-fame-w516550.

37. Quoted in Chris Parton, "Natalie Maines Is Still Not Ready to Make Nice," *CMT News*, March 11, 2015. www.cmt.com/news/1751742/natalie-maines-is-still-not-ready-to-make-nice.

Chapter Seven:
Changing with the Times

38. Dicaire, *The New Generation*, p. 223.

39. Steve Huey, "Lucinda Williams: *Car Wheels on a Gravel Road*," AllMusic, accessed on May 22, 2018. www.allmusic.com/album/car-wheels-on-a-gravel-road-mw0000028744.

40. Stephen Thomas Erlewine, "Toby Keith: *Shock'n Y'All*," AllMusic, accessed on May 22, 2018. www.allmusic.com/album/shockn-yall-mw0000208598.

41. Quoted in CMT.com Staff, "Toby Keith's USO Tour Underway," *CMT News*, April 26, 2011. www.cmt.com/news/1662677/toby-keiths-uso-tour-underway.

42. Quoted in Will Hodge et al, "10 New Country Artists You Need to Know: May 2017," *Rolling Stone*, May 9, 2017. www.rollingstone.com/country/lists/10-new-country-artists-you-need-to-know-may-2017-w481172.

43. Quoted in Hodge et al, "10 New Country Artists."

44. Quoted in Hodge et al, "10 New Country Artists."

45. Quoted in Hodge et al, "10 New Country Artists."

Essential
Albums

Publisher's note: Some albums may contain strong language or explicit content.

Alabama
Mountain Music (1982)

Buck Owens and the Buckaroos
I've Got a Tiger by the Tail (1965)

The Byrds
Sweetheart of the Rodeo (1968)

Carrie Underwood
Play On (2009)

Dixie Chicks
Fly (1999)

Dolly Parton
Jolene (1973)

Emmylou Harris
Wrecking Ball (1995)

Garth Brooks
Garth Brooks (1989)

George Strait
Ocean Front Property (1987)

Hank Williams
Hank Williams Sings (1951)

Johnny Cash
At Folsom Prison (1968)

The Judds
Why Not Me (1984)

Keith Urban
Fuse (2013)

Kenny Chesney
When the Sun Goes Down (2004)

Kenny Rogers
The Gambler (1978)

Little Big Town
Pain Killer (2014)

Loretta Lynn
Van Lear Rose (2004)

Merle Haggard and the Strangers
Mama Tried (1968)

Miranda Lambert
Four the Record (2011)

Nitty Gritty Dirt Band
Will the Circle be Unbroken (1972)

Patsy Cline
Sentimentally Yours (1962)

Trisha Yearwood
Everybody Knows (1996)

Reba McEntire
For My Broken Heart (1991)

Willie Nelson
Always on My Mind (1982)

Shania Twain
Come on Over (1997)

For More
Information

Books

Lusted, Marcia Amidon. *Blake Shelton: Country Singer and TV Personality*. Minneapolis, MN: Essential Library, 2015.
> This biography looks at the music of Blake Shelton, as well as his role on television. It explores his developing career and his charity work.

Ray, Michael, and David Lasky. *Alternative, Country, Hip-Hop, Rap and More: Music from the 1980s to Today*. New York, NY: Britannica Educational Publishers, 2012.
> This book covers various styles of popular music from the 1980s to the present, including country music.

Watson, Stephanie. *Keith Urban: Award-Winning Country Star*. Minneapolis, MN: Essential Library, 2015.
> Watson's book explores the life and career of country and western star Keith Urban.

Willett, Edward. *Johnny Cash: Fighting for the Underdog*. New York, NY: Enslow Publishing, 2018.
> Willett's biography explores the Man in Black's struggle with poverty, loss, and drug addiction. It explores how Cash hit bottom—and then rose up to have a successful career.

Young, Frank, and David Lasky. *The Carter Family: Don't Forget this Song*. New York, NY: Harry N. Abrams, 2012.
> This book tells the story of the first family of country music and how they changed the concept of this genre of music.

Websites

Academy of Country Music (ACM)

www.acmcountry.com

> Based in California, the ACM was founded in 1964 to promote country music in the western states, mainly the Bakersfield sound pioneered by Buck Owens, Merle Haggard, and others. The group's website is largely dedicated to the prestigious ACM Awards show and includes photos, videos, news, and information about the biggest country stars of the day.

Country Music Association (CMA)

www.cmaworld.com

> The CMA was founded in 1958 as a trade organization to promote country music throughout the world. Its website features wide coverage of country music news, events, awards shows, festivals, and artist biographies.

Country Music Television (CMT)

www.cmt.com

> CMT's official website features country music news, artist biographies, thousands of music videos, and replays of the channel's popular shows.

Nash Country Daily

www.nashcountrydaily.com

> This contemporary country music website offers stories, podcasts, and daily and weekly email newsletters to keep fans updated on anything and everything country.

Taste of Country

tasteofcountry.com/category/country-music-news

> This website features breaking news stories about country music and performers, as well as up-to-date concert information and current interviews with some of country music's biggest stars.

Index

Picture
Credits

Cover (main, background) DigtialStorm/iStock/Thinkstock; pp. 7, 33 Courtesy of the Library of Congress; p. 8 Debby Wong/Shutterstock.com; p. 11 Robert Alexander/Archive Photos/Getty Images; p. 13 Paul Fearn/ Alamy Stock Photo; pp. 14, 34 Elmer Williams/Country Music Hall of Fame and Museum/Getty Images; p. 19 AP Photo/Alan Marler; p. 21 Archive Photos/Getty Images; p. 22 Silver Screen Collection/Getty Images; p. 26 Photo Courtesy of Greg Tutmarc; p. 28 Bob Wills Photo by Michael Ochs Archives/ Getty Images; pp. 37, 56, 68, 73 David Redfern/Redferns/Getty Images; p. 38 Alabama Department of Archives and History; p. 41 GAB Archive/ Redferns/Getty Images; pp. 45, 50 Michael Ochs Archives/Getty Images; p. 48 Michael Mauney/The LIFE Images Collection/Getty Images; p. 52 Merle Haggard Photo by Michael Ochs Archives/Getty Images; p. 57 National Archives Archeological Site/Wikimedia Commons; p. 61 Paul Natkin/ Getty Images; p. 63 Peter Simon/Getty Images; p. 67 Hulton Archive/Getty Images; p. 75 Time Life Pictures/DMI/The LIFE Picture Collection/Getty Images; p. 79 Anthony Pidgeon/Redferns/Getty Images; p. 81 C Flanigan/ FilmMagic/Getty Images; p. 85 Alli Harvey/WireImage/Getty Images; p. 88 Mat Hayward/Shutterstock.com; back cover kzww/Shutterstock.com.

About
the Author

Tamra B. Orr is an author living in the Pacific Northwest with her family. She has written more than 500 nonfiction books for readers of all ages. Orr graduated from Ball State University with a degree in secondary education and found that she would rather write about the world than anything else. Her limited spare time is spent writing letters, reading books, and going tent camping throughout her state. She listens to music every single minute she is working and admits that country music takes up a significant portion of her playlist. She is grateful to have learned about new artists to add to her favorite songs.